D0343449

A Guide for the Young Economist

William Thomson

The MIT Press
Cambridge, Massachusetts
London, England

© 2001 Massachusetts Institute of Technology

All rights reserved. No part of this book may be reproduced in any form by any electronic or mechanical means (including photocopying, recording, or information storage and retrieval) without permission in writing from the publisher.

This book was set in Palatino by Interactive Composition Corporation (LATEX).

Printed and bound in the United States of America.

Library of Congress Cataloging-in-Publication Data

Thomson, William, 1949–
    A guide for the young economist / William Thomson.
       p.   cm.
    Includes bibliographical references.
    ISBN 0-262-20133-X (alk. paper) — ISBN 0-262-70079-4 (pbk.: alk. paper)
    1. Economics—Research. 2. Economics—Authorship. 3. Academic writing. I. Title.

 H62.T465   2001
 808′.06633—dc21   00-064588

To Suzanne

Contents

Preface

This book consists of three essays offering advice to young economists working on their dissertations, preparing their first papers for submission to a professional journal, getting ready to give their first presentation at a conference or a job seminar, or facing their first refereeing assignment.

The division of the work into three chapters on writing papers, giving talks, and writing referee reports is somewhat arbitrary. Most advice on writing well also applies to speaking well; and the criteria for evaluating a paper for journal publication are, of course, relevant to writing one's own papers. Thus the three essays inevitably overlap. Nevertheless, there are enough issues that relate specifically to each activity to justify the separation. Also, having been written on different occasions, the three chapters differ in style and tone—a variety I hope will make them more interesting to read.

The way we write or speak is largely a matter of taste. In a number of cases, I could well imagine that you, the reader, will make a different choice from the one I suggest. Therefore, if I use the imperative mode extensively, it is only because preceding each piece of advice with an apology would have been tiresome. What is most important is that you become aware of the issues. How you resolve each of them should be the result of a deliberate decision made with the specific application and particular audience in mind. However, if I have no intention of mounting the barricades to uphold my position on punctuation at the end of displayed formulae, I certainly would take up arms in defense of clarity, simplicity, and unity. "I like what is structured, clear and concise" (Henri Tomasi, composer, 1909–1971), and I hope you do too.

It is, of course, with some trepidation that I publish advice on writing. I can't help wondering how many of my own recommendations I have violated herein. With luck I will have the opportunity to revise the book for a second edition and eliminate some of its imperfections. This is a task I will not be able to accomplish on my own. Please write to me. I must have omitted issues you care about. And you will almost certainly disagree with some of my advice. Moreover, the essays would be enriched by a discussion of problems specific to areas other than those I am familiar with. I invite you to send me suggestions for expanding the scope of the essays to make them better guides to writing and speaking about other subjects. `wth2@troi.cc.rochester.edu`

Acknowledgments

I have received help from many readers, and I gratefully acknowledge their contributions.

For "Writing Papers," I thank Marcus Berliant, John Chipman, Young-sub Chun, Jacques Crémer, Eddie Dekel, John Duggan, Stanley Engerman, James Foster, Yannis Ioannides, Biung-Ghi Ju, Tarık Kara, Jerry Kelly, Bettina Klaus, Ralph Locke, Kin Chung Lo, Leslie Marx, Lionel McKenzie, Philip Reny, Suzanne Scotchmer, Jean-Max Thomson, and Jong-Shin Wei. I thank James Schummer for making a reality of my fantasy of letters tumbling down a cliff in accordance with the laws of physics (footnote 18), using the LATEX rotating package by Leonor Barroca. I thank Toru Hokari for some of the figures and Christopher Colton for giving life to my primitive cartoons ideas. My greatest debt is to Martin Osborne, James Schummer, John McMillan, and John Pencavel. An early version of the essay appeared in the *Journal of Economic Literature* 37 (1999): 157–83 under the title "The Young Person's Guide to Writing Economic Theory," and I thank the *Journal* for permission to use this material. I am also indebted to two anonymous referees of the *Journal* for their numerous suggestions.

For "Giving Talks," I thank Stanley Engerman, Ronald Jones, and Jean-Max Thomson for their remarks, and Jean-Pierre Benoît and Martin Osborne for many extremely useful comments.

For "Writing Referee Reports," I thank Stanley Engerman and François Maniquet for their comments, and Jacques Crémer, Dan Hamermesh, Jerry Kelly, John McMillan, Martin Osborne, John Weymark, and Michael Wolkoff for numerous suggestions.

I thank Biung-Ghi Ju for providing the illustrations for the color insert.

For the artwork on the cover, I thank Dimitri Thomson.

Finally, I have greatly benefited from the comments of a team of anonymous reviewers for the MIT Press.

1 Writing Papers

Here are my recommendations for writing better papers. The essay addresses general issues of presentation and in its details is mainly concerned with methods of describing and manipulating formal models, not with writing up empirical work. However, as most articles begin with the introduction and analysis of a model, I hope the points I make here will be useful to all economists, irrespective of their fields—not just to fledgling theorists.

The principles of good writing—simplicity, clarity, unity—are universal, but putting them into practice almost always offers several choices, and advice unavoidably reflects personal tastes. Also, my recommendations will occasionally be incompatible or inappropriate for your particular paper. Judgment is needed. Exercise yours.

Clear exposition requires revising, revising, and revising again. Undoubtedly, you will spend many months perfecting your first papers, but this work is one of the wisest investments you will ever make. In the future, you will face the same issues again and again, and the experience you will have accumulated will help you handle them more and more efficiently.

Do not assume that if your ideas are interesting, you will be read whether or not you write well. Your paper is competing for attention with many others that constantly land on the desks of the people you hope to reach. If they cannot see at a glance that they will gain something from reading it, they will not even start.

Finally, putting your results on paper is not subsidiary to producing them. The process of writing itself always leads to new knowledge. Learn to write but also write to learn.[1]

---

1. I borrowed this formula from William Zinsser's 1988 book, which I strongly recommend.

1   General Principles

Clarity should be your principal objective, and everything you do should be directed toward achieving it. No one will read very far into a paper if it is a burden. Make your paper inviting and convey your message efficiently. Be both precise and concise. However, I do not have a particular recommendation on how long a paper should be except for "Make it as long as it needs to be: no longer and no shorter." If its structure is clear, length will not be a problem.[2]

1.1   Write So That You Will Not Have to Be Read

By leafing through the article, a reader should be able to spot easily your main findings, figure out most of the notation, and locate the crucial definitions needed to understand each formal result.

A reader who has found your central point interesting and wants to know more about it but has little time to invest in your work (no-one has several free hours to devote to it) should be able to grasp the novel aspects of your model, your estimation technique, or your method of proof by visual inspection—without actually reading the paper. A lot can be learned from a well-written argument by just glancing at the way it is structured and identifying the central assumptions and the known theorems on which it is based.

Think about the way you read a paper yourself. You probably do not proceed in a linear way. Instead, you scan it for the results and look around them for an explanation of any notation and terminology you do not recognize or cannot guess.[3] You do not like hunting for the information. Your readers have better things to do too.

1.2   Don't Forget How You Made Your Discoveries

In presenting your work, draw lessons from the process that led you to your discoveries. You do not have to reproduce this process in your

2. Even though this essay is much longer than the average paper, not all papers—except in Lake Woebegone—can be shorter than average.

3. At least, this is how you will learn to read, and this is certainly the way your professors would like you to read: look for the main message of the contribution and the general idea of the proofs, and avoid getting bogged down in the details of the model or of the proofs.

paper, but it is sometimes worth telling your readers a little about it. In a seminar presentation especially, you can sometimes do more because of the informality of these occasions and because a didactic tone is more acceptable there than in a journal article. An explanation of how you arrived at the formulation of your problem and at your results should not, however, be a license to present a rambling discussion mixing notation, definitions, assumptions, and goals like the ingredients of a big salad. Even worse is adding some semiformal algebraic manipulations (tossing the salad?), and suddenly confronting us with: "We therefore established the following result ... " As a reader, I feel as if I've been mugged when that happens.

When finished, your paper will cover an arbitrary number of goods and agents, general production possibilities, uncertainty, and so forth—and nobody will understand it. If you read it several months later, you will not understand it either. You arrived at your main theorem in small steps—by first working it out for two agents, two goods, and linear technologies, with no uncertainty and by drawing lots of diagrams. It is also by looking at simple versions of your model that your readers will understand the central ideas. Most likely it is these central ideas, not the details of your proofs, that will help them in their own work.

1.3 Don't Forget Your Errors

There is nothing like having misunderstood something to really understand it; and there is nothing like having seriously misunderstood it to really, really understand it. Instead of being embarrassed by your errors, cherish them. I would even say that you cannot claim to understand something completely until you very thoroughly understand the various ways in which it can be misunderstood. It has been said before, and better: *"Erreur, tu n'es pas un mal."*

Your readers are likely to fall victim to the same misunderstandings you did. Remembering where you had trouble will let you anticipate where you may lose them and help you give better explanations. In a seminar, quickly identifying the reason why someone in the audience is confused about an aspect of your paper may prevent a ten-minute exchange that could force you to rush through the second half of your presentation.

1.4 Demonstrate the Originality and Significance of Your Contribution

Show that what you did has not been done before and that your conclusions are not direct consequences of known results. Explain how your assumptions differ from those used in related literature and why these are important differences, conceptually and technically. Cite the relevant articles and tell readers how they pertain to your subject.

Explain what motivated you in your investigation, but do not over-explain or your readers will become suspicious.

When arguing for the significance of your results, great is the temptation to present them with the utmost generality, with big words and in gory detail. Resist it! Try instead to make your reasoning appear simple, even trivial. This exercise in humility will be good for your soul. It will also give referees a warm feeling about you. And most important, it will actually help you prove your results at the next level of generality.

It is unfortunate that the trade-off between the space devoted to an article in a journal and the time readers need to understand it is so routinely resolved in favor of saving space. Frequently, the refereeing process and the constraints of publication have the effect of eliminating from a paper much of what could make it easily comprehensible. This may lead you to think that if your article does not contain at least one difficult-looking result it is not ready for submission. Of course, you are rightly proud of the sophisticated reasoning that has led you to your findings. Nevertheless, work hard to make them look simple.[4]

1.5 Understand the Function of Each Component of Your Paper

Think carefully about how each part of your paper fits with the others.

Your *title* should be as descriptive of your content as possible. Although most titles simply announce the subject, sometimes a title may also describe the result. Is that possible in your case? Is it desirable? "On the Number of Competitive Equilibria," for example, tells you what the paper is about, whereas "The Number of Competitive Equilibria Is Odd" essentially states its result. Often it is not possible to preview the main message of your paper so compactly, but it is always worth trying to do so.

---

4. As a young economist, it is natural for you to feel proud of the complicated things you achieve. As you get older, you will become proud of the simple things you do—but not because you will no longer be able to handle the complicated things!

Devote attention to your *abstract*, as many potential readers or listeners will decide whether to become actual readers or attend your presentation on the basis of the abstract. Keep in mind that abstracts are also meant to be published and read separately from the paper itself. They appear in the *Journal of Economic Literature* and may be reproduced in the book of abstracts given to the conference participants, on the web page of the conference, or in the proceedings volume. List *keywords* for the paper in order of declining importance. If they do not all appear in your abstract, something is wrong: you need to revise the list, or rewrite your abstract, or both. Also, if the first three or four keywords are not part of your title, there should be good reasons for their absence.

In writing your *acknowledgments,* be generous. Include the seminar participant who came up with a particularly apt name for a condition you introduced or directed you to pertinent references. However, you should apportion credit among the various people who helped you commensurately with the usefulness of their comments and the time and effort they expended on your work. The anonymous referee who sent you five pages of suggestions certainly deserves recognition in a separate sentence. In some cases, you may ask the journal editor whether the referee is willing to be identified.

The *introduction* to the paper should place your work in the context of the existing literature on the topic and describe your principal findings. Do not, however, start with a two- or three-page survey of the field; your reader will want to know about your own contribution sooner than that. Your language should be as plain as possible, and you should skip the details at this point. If you have to refer to an important concept whose formal definition is too technical for an introduction, put the term between quotation marks. This convention signals readers they need not worry if there are not acquainted with it as you've used it and that you will explain it later.

Your *review of the literature* on which you build should not be a mere enumeration of earlier articles. Give priority to the development of the ideas rather than describing the history of your subject blow by blow, although who did what and when should be included, and it should be unambiguously clear where you stepped in, as illustrated in section 1.6 below.

The *body* of the paper need not repeat all the points you made in the introduction, but some reiteration is unavoidable. As for proofs, I do not generally favor relegating them to appendices (see section 5.6).

Your *conclusion* should not be a rehash of the introduction. A compact summary of your results and a statement of the main lessons to be drawn from your analysis, however, are a good lead in to a general discussion of promising directions for future work and, perhaps, a list of specific questions to be explored. A table summarizing your results, or, more generally, comparing the critical assumptions and main conclusions of your work and earlier papers on the subject may be very useful.

In your *bibliography*, in addition to the specific papers your work generalizes, cite the relevant background literature. If a good survey of the subject is available, mention it. If you discover that they are relevant, you may have to list certain papers that you did not use, even papers you came across after you completed your own. One of them may contain results that you discovered independently; in that case, you will need to rewrite your paper to focus it on what is truly new. If your assumptions are not exactly the same as those of the other writer— they rarely are—or if your methods of proof differ, your efforts will not have been in vain. The overlap certainly will lessen the interest of your paper, and you may have to delete the overlapping materials. If you choose to keep them, acknowledge the other author's priority, note that you obtained your results independently, and explain how they still add to knowledge of the subject.

Finally, check your *references* carefully (the title of the latest version of a paper you cite may be different from the title of the version you used), and update them as these papers are published.

The structure of your paper should be clear, as should the structure of each section, subsection, and paragraph. A good way to see how your paragraphs fit together is to summarize each one in a sentence. Does the string of these sentences make sense? It should. Perform this exercise also at the level of subsections, and then sections. But remember that readers will not have the benefit of these summaries. Make sure that the structure of the paper is clear *to them* from what they see on the page.

1.6   *In the Literature Review, Tell a Story—Don't Enumerate*

Below is an illustration of the difference between an introduction that simply enumerates other authors' findings—and bores the reader—and one that tells the story of how a succession of researchers brought us progressively closer and closer to the resolution of an important mystery; one more step, yours perhaps, and the mystery is completely solved.

Enumeration Author 1 shows that on the domain of all games satisfying Condition 1, Nash equilibrium is not guaranteed to exist. Author 2 shows that on the domain of games satisfying Condition 2, existence may not hold either. On the domain of games satisfying Condition 3 and in the two-player case, Author 3 shows existence. Here, we investigate the case of three or more players under Condition 3.

Narrative On the domain of all games satisfying Condition 1, Nash equilibrium is not guaranteed to exist (Author 1). Since in applications payoff functions usually satisfy certain restrictions not implied by Condition 1, the question arose whether nonexistence of equilibrium persists when these restrictions are imposed. Unfortunately yes, at least for payoff functions satisfying Condition 2 (Author 2). This condition is frequently met, as it is equivalent to production functions exhibiting decreasing returns to scale; decreasing returns to scale are typical of the industrial sector that is a concern of this paper. Of course, if returns to scale decrease "sufficiently fast," payoff functions may satisfy the strong form of Condition 2 known as Condition 3. Recent empirical work suggests that Condition 3 may, indeed, often be met. Is existence recovered under this condition? The answer is yes, but for technical reasons discussed below it is known only in the case of two firms (Author 3). Our goal in this paper is to resolve the issue in the case of three or more firms.[5]

2   Notation

When you are in the middle of an exciting discovery, you probably do not stop to ponder notation; as a result, your variables are whatever first comes to mind. When writing up your results, however, this is not the notation you should use. Bad notation can make an otherwise well-written paper impossible to read.

2.1   *Learn LATEX or a Related Program*

One of your first professional choices will be what typesetting software to use. I strongly endorse LATEX (or TEX, or Scientific Word, whichever one you handle best). LATEX makes plain text look beautiful and, because it "understands" the structure of mathematical expressions, it has immeasurable benefits for the writing of proofs. Moreover, as it is

---

5. A difference between these two introductions is that the second puts authors' names in parentheses, placing the major focus on the results rather than on who established them.

so widely used (in mathematics, it has truly become the typesetter's ${\rm \LaTeX}{\rm_I}{\rm N}$), you will find it very convenient when collaborating with coauthors around the world.[6]

If you do not know how to use these software programs, ask one of your younger classmates to teach you. (Knowledge about computers goes from the young to the old.)

These programs will give you considerable freedom in developing your own style. When submitting a paper to a journal, however, respect its guidelines—and do not get carried away.[7] To emphasize certain aspects of your paper, such as important terminology or, on a rare occasion, when explaining a critical fact or a central conclusion, you should certainly exploit typographical choices you have (such as italics). But if *everything **IS** emphasized, NOTHING **IS**!*

Also, use a spellchequer.

2.2 *Choose Easily Recognizable Notation*

The best notation is notation whose meaning can be guessed. Of course, after working on your paper for several months, you have no problem remembering what all your variables designate. Unfortunately, what you call x is what your reader has been calling m since graduate school.

When you see a man walking down the street carrying a baguette under his arm and wearing a beret, you do not have to be told that he is a Frenchman. You know he is. You can immediately and legitimately invest him with all the attributes of Frenchness, which greatly facilitates the way you think and talk about him. You can guess his children's names—Renée or Edmond—and chuckle at his supposed admiration for Jerry Lewis.

Similarly, if Z designates a set, call its members z and z', or perhaps x and y, which are z's neighbors in the Latin alphabet. But don't call them b nor ℓ. Upon encountering z and z', your reader will know immediately what space they belong to, how many components they have, that these components are called z_i and z'_j, and so on. If Φ is a family of functions, reserve the notation φ and $\tilde{\varphi}$, (perhaps ψ) for members of the family, but don't use α or m.

---

6. Readers of an earlier version of this essay suggested that I recommend the *$\LaTeX$ Graphics Companion* by Goosens, Rahtz, and Mittelbach (1997) and *PSTricks* by Timothy van Zandt (1997).

7. Journals that request electronic files find it harder to work with a heavily styled document.

Figure 1.1
Use Notation That Makes Sense. A set contains its elements, so designate it by a letter bigger than those used for the elements: "$a \in A$" is believable; "$A \in a$" is not. Lots of a's can fit in A, but if you insist on stuffing A's and B's into a, you will break something.

If R_i is agent i's preference relation, you may have to designate his most preferred bundle in some choice set by $b_i(R_i)$, his demand correspondence by $d_i(R_i)$, and so on, but dropping this functional dependence may not create any ambiguities. You may write b_i and d_i, provided you designate agent j's most preferred element in her choice set and her demand correspondence by b_j and d_j, and the comparable concepts when agent i's preferences are changed to R_i' by b_i' and d_i'.

By the way, the word *if* is often used to introduce notation, as I did above ("If R_i is agent i's preference relation"); but a definitional *if* may be ambiguous, especially in the middle of a proof. When you write "If x is the Walrasian allocation of e," the reader may think you are making a conditional statement about a previously introduced variable, instead of naming a new one. To avoid the problem, write "If x designates the Walrasian allocation of e, then ..." Alternatively, after defining W as the Walrasian correspondence, write "If $x \equiv W(e)$, then ..." or "Let $x \equiv W(e)$. Then ..."

Designate time by t, land by ℓ, alternatives by a, mnemonic notation by mn and so on (making sure that no two concepts in your paper start with the same letter).

Figure 1.2
The Notation ϵ Rarely Designates Large Quantities. It most often refers to a small quantity or a quantity that goes to zero.

People in your field may use certain letters to designate something so commonly that their interpretation may interfere with the way you want to use those letters. In that case, it is probably better to accept tradition. Do not, for instance, designate just any quantity by ϵ. Reserve this letter for small quantities or for quantities that end up being arbitrarily small.[8] (Incidentally, choosing $\{\epsilon^n\}$ for a sequence converging to zero as n goes to infinity is overdoing it. Use $\{1/n\}$, or speak of a certain statement being true for arbitrarily small ϵ.)

Similarly, I suggest that you call your generic individual i, with preference relation R_i or $\succeq_i$, utility function u_i, and endowment vector ω_i. The production set is Y. Prices are p, quantities are q. Calligraphic letters often refer to families of sets; so a is a member of the set A, which is chosen from the family $\mathcal{A}$. But these are just suggestions: do not be slave to any convention. In your application, calling individual i's endowment e_i may in fact make more sense than designating it ω_i. And it may be more convenient to refer to your individuals as agents or traders and to

---

8. I like the fragile look of my ϵ, especially when my printer is running out of toner. How could one doubt that the quantity it designates is about to fade into nothingness? However, as a referee reminded me, in econometrics the error term ϵ is not necessarily a small quantity but rather a quantity that one would *like* to be small.

use a or t as their generic names. If you give too many of your variables nonstandard names, however, take into account the cost to readers of having to deal with expressions that will end up looking very unfamiliar: if a is your notation for agents and e for endowments, agent a's endowment will be e_a, which they will not immediately recognize as ω_i.

2.3   Choose Mnemonic Abbreviations for Assumptions and Properties

Do not refer to your assumptions and properties by numbers, letters, or letter-number combinations.

If you describe Assumptions A1–A3 and B1–B4 on page 2, but don't state your first theorem until page 10, it will be virtually impossible for readers to remember them. But the fact that Assumptions *Diff*, *Mon*, and *Cont* refer to differentiability, monotonicity, and continuity will be obvious even to a reader starting there. Choose your abbreviations carefully: if you write *Con*, it may not be clear whether you mean continuity or convexity; so, write *Cont* or *Conv*. The cost to you is a mere keystroke, but it will save readers from a backward search for the property you mean. Admittedly, naming each assumption in a way that suggests its content is not always possible, especially in technical fields.

A common way to introduce an abbreviation for a condition is to place it in parentheses after the full name of the condition when it is first formally stated. This is fine, but when the abbreviation is used later on, the parentheses are no longer needed.[9]

Abbreviations can often be avoided altogether but if not, use them sparingly. Certainly, never put them in a section heading. Although many authors refer to axioms by numbers or abbreviations, I see no advantage to doing so. Numbers and abbreviations do save some space, but they will not shorten a twenty-page paper by more than five lines; and, mainly, they will not save time for your reader. And time is the commodity in short supply, not paper. I strongly recommend using different typeface (for instance, italics, or slanted type) for your axioms; they will stand out from the text and be perceived globally—as a unit, rather than being read syllable by syllable. Alternatively, you can achieve this important visual separation of the axioms from the text by capitalizing them, though I find this a less effective solution.

---

9. For the same reason, when you begin a proof, write Proof: and not (Proof:).

To recapitulate a number of the points made so far, here is a demonstration of progressively better and better ways to refer to the property of *consistency* in a proof:

By (C3), we conclude that ...	You do not need the parentheses.
By C3 ...	It is hard to remember what C3 is, as compared to C1, C2, or C4. Use mnemonic abbreviations.
By con ...	What does *con* stand for—*continuity* or *consistency*?
By cons ...	Now we can guess that it is *consistency*, but the truncated word *cons* looks odd. Parentheses might be helpful here.
By (cons) ...	On the other hand, if the condition is written out in full, the sentence will begin to look like a regular English sentence.
By consistency ...	Still, it would be useful to signal that *consistency* is a formal concept in the theory, not just a general idea, and certainly not what we understand by this term in ordinary language. Capitalizing the property would indicate this formal status.
By Consistency ...	Now, thanks to the capitalization, we are aware that Consistency is a formal concept. Also, the term stands out from the text, allowing us to see easily where the property is used in the proof: three times maybe, or maybe only once, at the end. In that case, there may be benefits to presenting the proof as a sequence of two lemmas, Lemma 1 and Lemma 2, with Consistency making its appearance only in Lemma 2. Lemma 1 is actually the beginning of Theorem 2, too, so you could appeal to it there also. Come to think of it, in Lemma 2, Converse Consistency would do just as well. So, follow Lemma 1 with two lemmas: Lemma 2 invokes Consistency, and Lemma 3 (better still, Lemma 2′, to show the parallelism with Lemma 2) invokes Converse Consistency.

By *consistency* ...   The switch from Consistency is mainly be-
                            cause italics will make the term stand out
                            more. Aesthetically, it is also little more pleas-
                            ing (to me); CONSISTENCY would be over-
                            doing the emphasis. Since italics are also a
                            common way of emphasizing a word, slanted
                            or oblique type may be a better choice here. A
                            disadvantage of slanted or oblique type, how-
                            ever, is that it does not stand out from regu-
                            lar typeface quite as much as italics does and
                            is not always easily distinguishable from the
                            latter.

2.4   Use Only Notation You Can Easily Pronounce or Draw on the Board

In choosing notation, keep in mind that you will give oral presentations
of your work and may want to write on a board. It is not immediately
clear how to read the sentence "I assume $\succeq_i$ and $\succeq_i'$ to be continuous
and monotonic." And how do you pronounce the special symbol you
just created with your newly acquired computer skills?

Capitalized script letters are hard to draw, and therefore hard for your
audience to read. Avoid them. Choose only notation you can easily reproduce (This advice is not as critical nowadays, thanks to transparencies.) If you can't distinguish between some of the Greek letters, avoid
them too. (By now, however, you should know the Greek alphabet. If
not, get your Greek classmates to coach you.)

If you are Japanese or Korean, don't use ℓ and r in the same paper;
if you are Greek, avoid Greek letters, since you will find it difficult to
mispronounce them correctly; if you are French, eliminate all words containing the *th* sound or beginning with the letter *h*. (Je plaisante, voyons!).

If you can't say *substitutability*, assume that the goods are comple-
ments instead—or give up on demand theory. If you have trouble with
heteroskedasticity, econometrics is not for you.

2.5   Don't Introduce Notation You Will Use Only Once or Twice

There is no point defining a new piece of notation if you hardly ever
refer to it. How often must a concept be used to deserve its own sym-

bol? Twice? Three times? I will let you decide. (But you will agree that notation that is never used is not needed.)

I feel the same way about utility notation when only preferences are involved. It is wonderful, of course, that preference relations satisfying certain properties can be represented by numerical functions, and these representations are sometimes useful or even necessary. Unfortunately, that has become a common excuse to use them even when they only clutter up the text. Suppose, for example, that you want to write that the allocation rule φ is *resource-monotonic*. This means that every agent i benefits from an increase in the social endowment. Then (here, I skip the quantifications), you can write "$u_i(\varphi_i(u, \Omega)) \geq u_i(\varphi_i(u, \Omega'))$," but is such an expression preferable to "$\varphi_i(R, \Omega)\ R_i\ \varphi_i(R, \Omega')$" or $\varphi_i(\succeq, \Omega) \succeq_i \varphi_i(\succeq, \Omega')$. If your paper involves long strings of such terms, as may well be the case, utility notation will contribute to giving it an unnecessarily messy appearance.

Matters are worse in the above example because, in discussions of certain normative issues of welfare economics, social choice, or public finance, utility functions often have cardinal significance—whereas the property I defined depends only on ordinal preferences. Even if your theory may only involve the underlying preference relations, some of your readers from a different tradition will be tempted to compare utilities, or equate them, or maximize their sum, and so on. On the other hand, if you are addressing a problem of demand theory and need to calculate matrices of partial derivatives, then you cannot, of course, avoid utility notation.

2.6   Respect the Hierarchy of the Different Parts of a Paper

Do not refer in the main text to terms, ideas, or derivations introduced in a footnote or in a remark, as the reader may have skipped it. There is a hierarchy here you have to respect. Footnotes should contain only information that is not essential to understanding your main argument.

I can see two exceptions to this rule. The first concerns your conventions for designating vector inequalities. Do not let readers guess or infer from the context what your inequality symbols mean. Define them the first time you use them. Doing so in a footnote is acceptable because it is a very common practice;[10] in fact, that's where most of us look for

---

10. The *New York Times* of August 14, 1996, contains a long article about the demise of the footnote, or at least the footnote as citation. It reports a major debate raging in academic publishing. It quotes Anthony Grafton (1997): "The philosopher Pierre Bayle [...]

them when we need them.[11] Alternatively, you can explain them in a preliminary section on notation.

The second exception is for sources of data used in your empirical study. Whether such sources are new is important information to researchers in the field, and sources are often provided in footnotes.

2.7 Choose Notation Resulting in Uncluttered Mathematical Expressions

Avoid unnecessary symbols.

Do not use multiple subscripts and superscripts if you can avoid them. If you have only two agents, call their consumption bundles x and y, with generic coordinates x_k and y_k (instead of x_1 and x_2, with coordinates x_{1k} and x_{2k}).

As the bounds of summation and integration are often—I agree, not always—unambiguous, there is then no need to indicate them. Do not write $\sum_{i=1}^{n} x_i$, $\sum_{i \in N} x_i$, $\sum_i x_i$, $\sum_N x_i$, or $\sum_{i=1,\ldots,n} x_i$ when in most cases $\sum x_i$ is perfectly clear. I assure you that when they encounter $\sum x_i$, your readers will unanimously assume that your sum is carried out over i when i runs over its natural domain.

Similarly, although the set consisting of agent i alone should be denoted $\{i\}$, if you need to refer to it several times, just omit the curly brackets—with an apology for the abuse of notation. If O designates a list of objects indexed by agents in the set N, you should refer to the shorter list from which the i-th component has been deleted as $O_{N\setminus\{i\}}$ (the projection of O onto the subspace relative to $N\setminus\{i\}$), but it has become standard to write O_{-i}. The shortcut is convenient and I used it in the previous subsection.

It sometimes helps to assign a numerical value to a generic variable in order to make it stand out and to help readers decipher statements involving many other generic variables. For instance, if you define $i \in N$

---

published an encyclopedia in 1697 all but bursting with footnotes (including footnotes on footnotes)\footnote {Here is a challenge for you TEXxies (Should I write TEX-ies instead? My model is "Trekkies"): How do you make "toenotes" (footnotes on footnotes)?} in which he sought to demonstrate that knowledge of the world could be accurate if scholars rigorously revealed their sources in footnotes." Also, "the longest footnote Professor Grafton found appeared in a book called 'The History of Northumberland' by John Hodgson published in 1840. It ran 165 pages." Personally, I love footnotes. Perhaps because in academic writing, they are often the only place where you find evidence of life.

11. $x \geqq y$ means $x_i \geq y_i$ for all i; $x \geq y$ means $x \geqq y$ and $x \neq y$; $x > y$ means $x_i > y_i$ for all i. You could also use $x \geq y$, $x > y$, and $x \gg y$.

to be such that for all $j \in N$, $\sum_{k \in N} x_{ik} \geq \sum_{k \in N} x_{jk}$, you may want to set $i = 1$. Later on, this allows you to simplify $\prod_{k \in N} y_{ij} \geq \prod_{k \in N} z_{ik}$ to $\prod y_{1k} \geq \prod z_{1k}$. But "let $i \in N$, say $i = 1$, be such that for all $j \in N$, $\sum_{k \in N} x_{1k} \geq \sum_{k \in N} x_{jk}$," does not read well, because the variable i is introduced only to be immediately replaced by something else (that is, there is no expression in which i appears). Therefore, write "let $i \in N$ be such that $\sum_{k \in N} x_{ik} \geq \sum_{k \in N} x_{jk}$. Without loss of generality, take $i = 1$."

Match notation used in proofs with notation used in definitions. If M and M' are the possible values of a variable appearing in a condition, do not choose M^1 and M^2 in the proof of the theorem in which they appear. If you have two agents, with preferences R_1 and R_2 and endowments ω_1 and ω_2, the notation M_1 and M_2 would be even worse, because it will make readers think that the subscripts also refer to the two agents. Use M and M', and make them play exactly the roles they play in the definition. For instance, if in the definition, $M' > M$, avoid $M > M'$ in your application.

If F is your generic notation for a solution to the bargaining problem, you can certainly refer to the Nash solution as F^N, and when you apply it to the problem (S, d) with feasible set S and disagreement point d, you will get $F^N(S, d)$. But why not simply designate the Nash solution by N? If you can choose the disagreement point to be the origin[12]—it is almost always without loss of generality—then ignore it in the notation. Altogether, you will calculate $N(S)$, a lighter expression than $F^N(S, d)$. Systematically search for such notational simplifications; your text will be much cleaner.

Suppose, for example, that you use v as generic notation for some variable, and that in a proof you establish the existence of a particular value of this variable for which a certain statement holds. You do not then necessarily need special notation for that value, such as $\bar{v}$ or v_0; you can still use v. In most cases, it will be clear that for the remainder of the proof you are not talking about a general v anymore but about that particular one. Of course, if that specific value appears in some other proofs, it is safer to introduce a notation for it.

If you present a series of economies illustrating the various ways in which equilibrium may fail to exist, and if you do not refer to these particular economies elsewhere, you need not number them e_1, e_2, and so on. Call your first example e, and discuss it. When you are finished

---

12. This specification will be legitimate if your theory is invariant with respect to choices of a zero for the utility functions.

with your example, the variable e becomes available again and you can refer to your second and subsequent examples as e too.

Having defined an economy—specifying a set N of consumers, a profile $(R_i)_{i \in N}$ of preference relations, a profile $(\omega_i)_{i \in N}$ of endowments, a set M of firms, and a profile $(Y_j)_{j \in M}$ of production sets—you may want to summarize all of this data as a list $(N, (R_i)_{i \in N}, (\omega_i)_{i \in N}, M, (Y_j)_{j \in M})$. But do not drag this huge parenthesis throughout your paper; you will look like a refugee bending under the weight of his belongings. As most of what is in the parenthesis is fixed throughout your analysis, you can keep it in the background. This "maintained notation" is the counterpart of the "maintained assumptions," which are listed once, at the beginning. You could introduce a notation for the list—e for instance—but it depends on how much of the data in the parenthesis is fixed. If you are studying an implementation problem, in which the only critical data are the unknown preferences of the consumers, provide your notation for the set of agents, their endowments, the set of firms, their technologies, and so on (you will need it); but then describe an economy simply in terms of its preference profile $R \equiv (R_i)_{i \in N}$, obviating the need to introduce another notation such as e. Now you are a cheerful hiker coming down the hill, and readers will hardly notice the little backpack in which you carry your lunch.

Imagine that you are on a diet and that each symbol is worth one calorie. You will quickly discover that you can do with half as many. You will improve the readibility of your text and lose weight too.

3 Definitions

In this section, I discuss introducing, formatting, and sequencing definitions, as well as the issue of naming concepts.

3.1 Don't Assume Readers' Familiarity with Your Terms and Definitions

Define the terms you use, even those that you can legitimately assume everyone has already seen. There is rarely complete agreement on definitions in the literature. Different people understand even apparently standard, common terms like *core*, *public goods*, and *incentive compatibility* in different ways. So define them. The word *rationality* also frequently appears in formal developments in game theory without a definition. Do not make that mistake.

3.2   *Make It Clear When You Are Defining a New Term*

When you first use a term, make it immediately clear that it is indeed new. Do not let readers think they might have missed a definition given earlier, or that you assume they know the definition. Here are three possible ways of introducing a definition.

A function is *monotone* if . . .

A function is "monotone" if . . .

A function is said to be *monotone* if . . .

Most editors prefer the first format, and I use it throughout this essay. Its phrasing is direct, and the use of a different typeface helps readers retrieve the definition by simply scanning the paper, if needed. Although I find boldface or boldface italics best in this regard—and preferable to italics or plain text between quotation marks (neither of which makes the new terms stand out sufficiently)—I agree that boldface italics are not aesthetically pleasing. You should probably display the crucial definitions separately and you may precede each of them by the word **Definition** in boldface or in small capital letters (see the examples below). But do not introduce all definitions in this way, especially if there are many of them, as it will get tedious.

If you don't use special typography when you introduce new terms readers may assume that you are describing an implication of the term instead of defining it. Consider for example the sentence "an allocation rule is efficient if either it assigns to all agents amounts that are no greater than their peak amounts, or it assigns to all agents amounts that are not smaller than their peak amounts." Should it be read as an implication of the notion of efficiency they remember from their textbooks? Or is it a useful implication—perhaps an equivalent restatement—of this property in the context of the particular model under study?

To avoid repeating quantifications shared by several definitions you can group these definitions and state the quantification once, at the beginning. Factor them out, so to speak: "An allocation rule is *efficient* if for all preference profiles R and all allocations z that it selects for R, there is no allocation z' that all agents find at least as desirable as z and that at least one agent prefers; it is *weakly efficient* if instead there is no other allocation z' that all agents prefer to z."

3.3 Indicate the Kind of Mathematical Object Each New Notation Designates

When presenting a piece of notation, specify right away the kind of mathematical object it is: that is, whether it is a point in a vector space, a set, a function, or something else.

Do not write, "A pair (p, x) is a *Walrasian equilibrium* if ..." Instead, first define the price simplex $\Delta^{\ell-1}$ in the ℓ-dimensional Euclidean space and the allocation space X; then write "A pair $(p, x) \in \Delta^{\ell-1} \times X$ is a *Walrasian equilibrium* if ..."

Indicating explicitly the nature of the objects introduced is especially important if readers may not be familiar with them. For instance, writing "A triple $(\pi, x, y) \in \Delta^{(\ell-1)n} \times \mathbb{R}_+^{(m-\ell)n} \times \mathbb{R}^\ell$ is a *Lindahl equilibrium* if ..." helps them realize that π has components indexed by agents (these components are the Lindahl individualized prices).

By the way, a sequence of elements of X is not a subset of X but a function from the natural numbers to X. So, you cannot write $\{x^k\}_{k\in\mathbb{N}} \subseteq X$, nor can you write $\{x^k\}_{k\in\mathbb{N}} \in X$. Speak instead of "the sequence $\{x^k\}$ of elements of X," or of "the sequence $\{x^k\}$ where for all $k \in \mathbb{N}$, $x^k \in X$."[13]

3.4 Give Examples Illustrating Novel Definitions

Provide illustrative examples with your definitions, especially those likely to be unfamiliar to readers, as good exposition usually goes back and forth between the general and the particular. So, state each definition in general terms and then illustrate it. If you are defining a property that an object may or may not satisfy, give examples of

1. Objects that satisfy the definition;
2. Objects that do not satisfy the definition;
3. Objects that satisfy the definition but almost do not;
4. Objects that do not satisfy the definition but almost do.

Examples in Categories 3 and 4 are particularly important as they are responsible for three-fourths of the work involved in the proofs. Conversely, it may be precisely because they are covered by your theory that certain proofs can go through. In a paper, unfortunately, it is not easy to cite a range of examples that illustrates all four categories; but

---

13. Note that I dropped the $k \in \mathbb{N}$ subscript, which in most cases will be unnecessary.

it can sometimes be done in seminars, where adopting a didactic tone is more acceptable. In each case, choose objects that readers are more likely to have seen or that are more relevant to your analysis. Here are three more examples.

DEFINITION   A subset S of $\mathbb{R}^2$ is *convex* if for all $x, y \in S$ and all $t \in [0, 1]$, we have $tx + (1 - t)y \in S$.

In Figure 1.3, S_2 illustrates the notion of convexity better than S_1 does, because it forces your reader to realize that you do not mean strict convexity. Example S_3 is a little more subtle, because it is almost nonconvex (a point of its boundary having been removed). Example S_4 shows the typical way in which convexity is violated, and S_5 is a nonconvex set whose closure is convex (compare with S_3.)

DEFINITION   A function $f : \mathbb{R} \to \mathbb{R}$ is *increasing* if for all $t, t' \in \mathbb{R}$ with $t > t'$, we have $f(t) > f(t')$.

In Figure 1.4, f_1 and f_2 are dangerous illustrations of the notion of an increasing function because they may plant in the reader's mind the idea that your functions are concave, or perhaps linear. What you need is f_3, which shows the full generality of an increasing function: it has a kink, a convex part, a concave part, a discontinuity, and a horizontal tangency at one point. The function f_4 is useful too, as it shows a typical

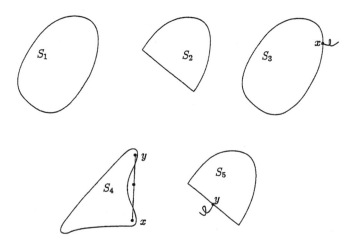

Figure 1.3
Examples of Convex Sets and Nonconvex Sets. The sets S_1 and S_2 are convex. So is S_3, although x has been removed from its boundary. The sets S_4 and S_5 are not convex; S_5 is also nonconvex because y has been removed from its boundary.

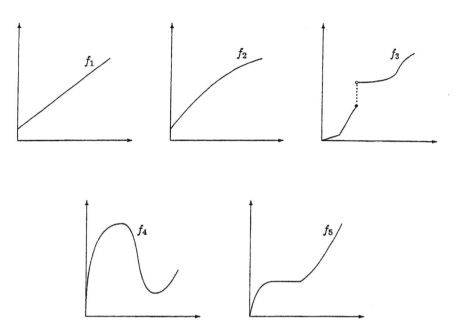

Figure 1.4
Examples of Increasing Functions and Functions That Are Not Increasing. Functions f_1, f_2, and f_3 are increasing. Functions f_4 and f_5 are not.

function that violates the property. The function f_5 is very important because it makes it clear that you want more of the function than it be nondecreasing.[14]

DEFINITION   The continuous preference relation R defined on $\mathbb{R}_+$, with asymmetric part P, is *single-peaked* if there exists $x^* \in \mathbb{R}_+$ such that for all $x, x' \in \mathbb{R}_+$ with either $x < x' \leq x^*$ or $x^* \leq x' < x$, we have $x'Px$.

Figure 1.5 presents the graphs of numerical representations of five preference relations. It is obvious that R_1 is single-peaked and that R_4 is not. But viewers may not immediately see R_2 as single-peaked because its representation achieves its maximum at an endpoint of its domain of definition; or they may see R_5 as single peaked, even though its representation has a plateau and not a peak. You should also make them aware that you include preferences that do not exhibit the symmetry illustrated by R_3 (there, two points that are symmetric with respect to

---

14. Several readers of this essay objected to sentences such as "this function is nondecreasing," which sounds too much like "this function is not a decreasing function," even though it means something else. Perhaps, we should speak of a "nowhere-decreasing function."

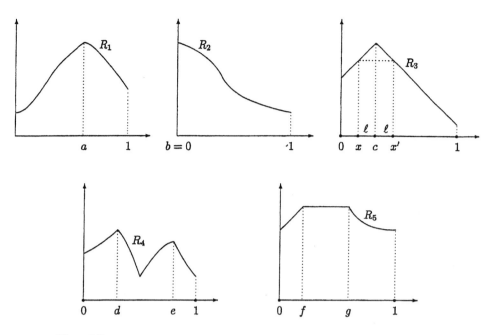

Figure 1.5
Single-Peaked Preference Relations and Non-Single-Peaked Relations. The graphs de-
pict functions representing preference relations defined on the interval [0, 1]. The relations
R_1 and R_2 are single-peaked, with peaks at a for R_1 and at b for R_2. The relation R_3 is
single-peaked too, but it is not sufficiently representative of the whole class, being symmetric with respect to the most preferred point, c. As readers who have not worked with
such preferences often assume that symmetry is part of the definition, you can include a
symmetric example—but only if you make it clear that most single-peaked preferences
do not have that property. The relations R_4 and R_5 are not single-peaked, as R_4 has two
local maxima, at d and e, and R_5 is maximized at any point of the nondegenerate interval
$[f, g]$.

the preferred point, such as x and x', are necessarily indifferent to each
other). Examples like these will be very useful to ensure that readers
perceive fully the boundary of your domain.

3.5 *Separate Formal Definitions from Interpretations*

As formal models can often be interpreted in several ways, it is very
useful to separate your formal description from the interpretation you
intend in your particular application. For example, after defining a domain V^n of n person coalitional games, you can write:

DEFINITION   A *solution on* $\mathcal{V}^n$ is a function that associates with every game $v \in \mathcal{V}^n$ a point $x \in \mathbb{R}^n$ such that $\sum x_i \leq v(N)$.[15]

and then explain:

If F is a solution on $\mathcal{V}^n$, v is a game in $\mathcal{V}^n$, and i is a player in N, the number $F_i(v)$ can be interpreted as the "value to player i of being involved in the game v—that is, the amount that the player would be willing to pay to have the opportunity to play it. Alternatively, it can be thought of as the amount that an impartial arbitrator would recommend that the player should receive.

The advantage of this separation is that it helps readers (and even yourself) discover the relevance of your results to other situations that they (and you) had not thought about initially. To pursue this example, remember that the theory of coalitional games overlaps greatly with the theory of cost allocation. A reader may be interested only in applications, not in abstract games, or perhaps does not care for the applications. You might catch the attention of such a reader by first giving general definitions and then pointing out the various possible interpretations of your model.

Another example is the class of *bankruptcy problems*. A bankruptcy problem is simply a point in the nonnegative quadrant of an $(n + 1)$-dimensional Euclidean space whose coordinates satisfy a certain inequality: that is, the sum of the first n numbers is greater than the last number. The first n coordinates are interpreted as the claims of n individuals on the net worth of a bankrupt firm, this worth being given as the last number. The inequality means that there is not enough to satisfy all the claims. This is why we call this a model of bankruptcy. The class of bankruptcy problems, however, is mathematically identical to an interesting class of problems in which the first n coordinates are the incomes of a group of taxpayers and the last number is the amount to be collected to cover the cost of some project; the same inequality is imposed, but its interpretation is different. It means that the sum of the incomes should be sufficient to finance the project.

---

15. Here we have a minor notational problem, as the n exponent to $\mathcal{V}^n$ indicates the n-player case, whereas the n exponent to $\mathbb{R}^n$ indicates the n-fold Cartesian product of $\mathbb{R}$ by itself. To avoid this problem, you could write $\mathcal{V}^{(n)}$, though I do not think the risk of confusion is sufficiently high to justify the parentheses.

3.6   Present Basic Concepts in Their Full Generality

As you will almost certainly use concepts that are meaningful far beyond the framework of your paper, you should first discuss and illustrate them without imposing the extra assumptions you will need
to invoke for your analysis. For example, when you define a Walrasian
equilibrium,[16] you should not assume convexity or monotonicity of preferences. Of course, these properties are relevant when you turn to the
issue of existence, but they have nothing to do with the general concept.
On the other hand, you probably will want to assume continuity of preferences, because specifying a noncontinuous example would take too
much space or time and would distract readers from the heart of the
definition.

Similarly, when you introduce a requirement on an allocation rule,
think about whether it would make sense if it were imposed on its own,
or whether it is mainly justified in the presence of other requirements.
If it is meaningful in and of itself, state it separately.

3.7   Write in Logical Sequences

Introduce terms in such a way that the definition of each new one involves only terms that have already been defined. Don't ask your readers
to wait until the end of the sentence or paragraph for clarification.

State the dimensionality of the commodity space before you introduce
consumers or technologies. In the standard model, a consumer is no
more than a preference relation defined over a subset of that space,
together with an endowment vector in the space; a technology is simply
a subset of the space. In each case, therefore, it is natural to specify the
space—that is, the number of goods—first. Thus, do not write: "$\mathcal{R}_{inc}$ is
the class of increasing preferences R, where by *increasing* is meant that
for all $x, y \in \mathbb{R}^{\ell}_{+}$ with $x \geq y$, we have $x \, R \, y$, ℓ being the dimensionality
of the commodity space." Instead write: "Let $\ell \in \mathbb{N}$ be the number of
goods. The preference relation R defined on $\mathbb{R}^{\ell}_{+}$ is *increasing* if for all
$x, y \in \mathbb{R}^{\ell}_{+}$ with $x \geq y$, we have $x \, R \, y$. Let $\mathcal{R}_{inc}$ be the class of increasing
preferences."

As another example, in which $\mathcal{R}^n$ denotes a domain of preference
profiles in an n-person economy, do not write:

---

16. The alternative phrase *competitive equilibrium* is often used instead.

DEFINITION   The social choice correspondence $F: \mathcal{R}^n \to A$ is *Maskin-monotonic* if for all R, $R' \in \mathcal{R}^n$ and all $a \in F(R)$, if for all $i \in N$, $L(R_i', a) \supseteq L(R_i, a)$, then $a \in F(R')$, where $L(R_i, a)$ and $L(R_i', a)$ are the lower contour sets of R_i and R_i' at a, with R and R' being profiles of preference relations defined over A, some alternative space, and Maskin being an economist at Princeton.

Instead write:

DEFINITION   Let Maskin be an economist at Princeton. Let A be a set of alternatives. Given R_i, a preference relation defined over A, and a, an alternative in A, let $L(R_i, a)$ be the lower contour set of R_i at a. The social choice correspondence $F: \mathcal{R}^n \to A$ is *Maskin-monotonic* if for all R, $R' \in \mathcal{R}^n$ and all $a \in F(R)$, if for all $i \in N$, $L(R_i', a) \supseteq L(R_i, a)$, then $a \in F(R')$.

Even better, introduce the basic notation first—you will use it elsewhere—and only then give the definition.[17] This separation will help highlight the essential idea underlying the concept.[18] Begin with: "Let A be a set of alternatives. Given R_i, a preference relation defined over A, and a, an alternative in A, let $L(R_i, a)$ be the lower contour set of R_i at a. Let $\mathcal{R}$ be a class of admissible preference relations defined over A. A *social-choice correspondence* associates with every profile of preference relations in $\mathcal{R}^n$ a non-empty subset of A."

Then, you can state the definition:

DEFINITION   The social-choice correspondence $F: \mathcal{R}^n \to A$ is *Maskin-monotonic* if for all R, $R' \in \mathcal{R}^n$ and all $a \in F(R)$, if for all $i \in N$, $L(R_i', a) \supseteq L(R_i, a)$, then $a \in F(R')$.

You may also want to display the hypothesis and the conclusion on separate lines:

DEFINITION   The social-choice correspondence $F: \mathcal{R}^n \to A$ is *Maskin-monotonic* if for all R, $R' \in \mathcal{R}^n$ and all $a \in F(R)$, if

$$\text{for all } i \in N, \ L(R_i', a) \supseteq L(R_i, a),$$

---

17. Note that the inverted construction of the first definition forces you to explain both $L(R_i', a)$ and $L(R_i, a)$, since the operator that gives for every preference relation—whether it be R_i or R_i'—and any alternative—whether it be a or b—the lower contour set of that preference relation at that alternative, has not been defined yet.
18. The same thing applies to propositions and theorems: do not introduce new notation in their statements.

then
$$a \in F(R').$$

If the hypotheses and the conclusions are simple enough, as they are in this example, displaying them may not be needed.

Some people will object to the double *if* in the condition as I wrote it. And it is awkward. Sometimes replacing one of two successive *if*s by something like *whenever* sounds a bit better, but here that substitution does not quite work. Another possible formulation is

$$L(R'_i, a) \supseteq L(R_i, a) \text{ for all } i \in N \text{ implies } a \in F(R').$$

There is yet one final option. It is a good one if you have made it clear that you are defining a property that your generic choice correspondence $F: \mathcal{R}^n \to A$ may or may not satisfy. (A possible drawback of this format is that it does not allow to number the definition, but it is not a serious one, as numbering definitions is rarely useful.)

MASKIN-MONOTONICITY   For all $R, R' \in \mathcal{R}^n$ and all $a \in F(R)$, if

$$\text{for all } i \in N, L(R'_i, a) \supseteq L(R_i, a),$$

then
$$a \in F(R').$$

Now return to the very first statement of the definition I gave and compare it to this last one. Which one do you like best?

Some writers recommend dropping the punctuation at the end of displayed formulas (for example, the hypothesis and the conclusion of the last statement of *Maskin-monotonicity*) on the principle that the indentation and centering serve as punctuation. There is no agreement about this convention, however, and I personally prefer my sentences to have a full complement of commas and periods.[19] (Editors will concur.)

Finally, make sure that the description in words of your definitions, or their components, match your formal statements. In an earlier version of

---

19. The period was recently celebrated by Antony Manguel (1999) as one of the major achievements of the millennium: "Diminutive as a mote of dust, a mere peck of the pen, a crumb on the keyboard, the full stop—the period—is the unsung legislator of our writing system." I could not agree more.

When my daughters were in primary school, I occasionally went with them to help with the kids' writing. My main job, as instructed by their teacher, was to check that every sentence they wrote began with a capital letter and ended with a period. I have learned my lesson well, and when I see a sentence that ends without a period, I experience the same queasiness I feel when I step too close to the edge of an open s this essay, I designated the "lower contour set of R_i at a" by $L(a, R_i)$—notation that seems standard in the field). But then I noticed that the order in which the phrase "lower contour set of R_i at a" refers to the two arguments of L did not match the order in which they are listed within the parenthesis. I chose to reorder them within the parenthesis because the "lower counter set at a of R_i" does not read as smoothly as the "lower counter set of R_i at a."

For the same reason, if you write "A feasible allocation is Pareto efficient if there is no other feasible allocation that all consumers find at least as desirable and that at least one consumer prefers," your formal definition should not be (using the notation I defined earlier for preferences and agents, and introducing $\mathcal{P}$ for the set of Pareto efficient allocations) "$z \in \mathcal{P}$ if (i) $z \in Z$ and (ii) for all $z' \in Z$ such that for some $i \in N$, $z'_i P_i z_i$, there is $j \in N$ such that $z_j P_j z'_j$." Write instead: "$z \in \mathcal{P}$ if (i) $z \in Z$ and (ii) there is no $z' \in Z$ such that for all $i \in N$, $z'_i R_i z_i$, and for some $j \in N$, $z'_j P_j z_j$."

3.8 Don't Collapse Two or Three Similar Statements into One

Compact definitions obtained by indicating the variants in parentheses may save space, but it does so at the cost of readers' time. Consider for example: "The function $f: \mathbb{R} \to \mathbb{R}$ is decreasing (increasing; nondecreasing) if for all $x, y \in \mathbb{R}$ with $x > y$, $f(x) < f(y)$ (respectively $f(x) > f(y)$; $f(x) \geq f(y)$)." The only way to be really sure we understand this triple definition is to read it three times (once for decreasing, once for increasing, and once for nondecreasing). Yet the definition itself is actually fairly simple. Grasping more complicated statements in that format requires unnecessarily exhausting mental gymnastics. Just restate the complete sentence for each of the various forms needed.

I also have a lot of trouble with *and/or* (or is it *or/and*?).

3.9 When Defining a Concept, Indicate What It Depends on

Do not write "The function f is *differentiable* at t if blah, blah, blah of t." Since what follows *if* depends on t, you should write "The function f is *differentiable at t* [including *at t* in the expression in italics if that is your typographical convention for definitions] if blah, blah, blah of t." You can then say "The function f is *differentiable* if it is differentiable at t for all t in its domain." A marginal rate of substitution is calculated at a point, so speak of agent i's *marginal rate of substitution at x_i*. For an example from the theory of implementation, speak of a *monotonic transformation of agent i's preferences at x_i*, and not just of a *monotonic transformation*.

My final example pertains to the theory of cooperative games and the notion of consistency; it involves, after solving a game v, imagining that some of the players leave the scene with their pay-offs and then reassessing the situation as seen by the remaining agents. In referring to the game faced by the agents who stay, do not speak simply of *reducing v*, as a well-defined reduction operation requires you to specify a subset of the initial set of players—you should of course specify this initial set—and some initial payoff vector. If N is the initial set of players and $\mathcal{V}^N$ the class of games in which they may be involved, speak of the *reduced game of $v \in \mathcal{V}^N$ with respect to the subgroup $N' \subset N$ and the payoff vector $x \in \mathbb{R}^N$*. Indicate this double dependence in the notation. I recommend something like $r_{N'}^x(v)$. The letter r reminds us of the reduction. The subscript N' refers to the subgroup; a subscript is quite appropriate, as projections on subspaces are commonly indicated by subscripts and the reduced game belongs to a subspace of games. The superscript x indicates the payoff vector initially chosen; a second subscript would be acceptable here too, particularly because there is no way to confuse the notation for a subgroup with the notation for a payoff vector. Finally, the reduction is performed on the initial game v, which is given as an argument. Again, this is a completely standard procedure.

When you define a variable as a function of old ones, it should appear on the left-hand side of the equality or identity symbol. For instance, if M has already been defined, and M' is introduced next—with a value equal to M—write "Let $M' = M$" and not "Let $M = M'$." It often looks better to introduce definition by $\equiv$, as in "Let $M' \equiv M$."

Similarly, if the object of a paragraph is to show that a newly introduced variable, x, is greater than some parameter a of the model, writing "therefore $x > a$" is preferable to "therefore $a < x$." But it depends. If the variables a and x appear at both ends of a string of inequalities all pointing to the left, and if there are good reasons for them to point to the left, it might be better not to reverse the order in which a and x appear in the conclusion.

3.10 Be Unambiguous and Consistent in Quantifications

Pay special attention to quantifications. Universal quantifications can be written as *for all, for any, for every,* and *for each; given* can also introduce an object taken arbitrarily from some set. I have seen proofs in which all five ways were used, and that did not look good. Choose one type of expression and stick with it.

Be particularly careful about *for any*. When you write "If for any $x \in X$, $f(x) > a \ldots$," it is not clear whether you mean "for all x" or "for some x." Here is a second example of an ambiguous quantification: if you write "For $i \in N$, let x_i be an arbitrary consumption bundle," do you mean that (1) you have chosen some agent i arbitrarily and for that agent some bundle x_i, or (2) for every agent i, you have chosen some bundle x_i?

Although *for all* is the standard way of reading ∀, when you use words instead of the symbol, *for each* is often a little better. Indeed, the expression *for all* seems to require the sentence to continue in the plural, but the meaning of the sentence may be clearer in the singular. In fact, the singular is often more precise than the plural. Compare "A strategy profile is a *Nash equilibrium* if players do not gain by switching to other strategies" to "A strategy profile is a *Nash equilibrium* if no player gains by switching to another strategy." The second formulation, obviously, does not cover the case of several players jointly switching, whereas the first formulation could be understood as stating that the strategy profile should be immune to coordinated defection as well. "For each and every agent" is no good either—unless your agents are double agents.

3.11   Don't Use Different Terms or Phrases for the Same Concept

The remaining subsections on definitions are devoted to naming issues.

Refer to a given concept by only one name or phrase. Choose one and stick with it even if you have several good choices. Also indicate (in parentheses next to your definition, or in a footnote) the other terms by which it is known in the literature. In your first discussion of the general idea, you may use different terms to vary the language and avoid repetitions repetitions, which admittedly do not sound very good; but once you have formally defined and baptized the concept, refer to it only by that name.

The terms *game*, *game form*, and *mechanism* are used by different authors to designate the same concept. Pick one, for example *game form*, and write "A *game form*[20] is a pair $(S, h) \ldots$" or a "*game form* (also known as a game or a mechanism)," thereby telling readers that you will use

---

20. The terms *game* or *mechanism* are sometimes used.

the phrase *game form* (because it is in italics, if italics is your convention for new definitions) but reminding them that the terms *mechanism* and simply *game* also appear in the literature. Writing "a mechanism (or *game form*)" would be confusing.

Do not populate your paper with *individuals*, *agents*, *persons*, *consumers*, and *players*. One species is enough. Or, have a reason to vary language: if, for example, you refer to your agents as *consumers* but need to say that "consumer i consumes commodity l," I would understand your using *agent* i as a secondary term reserved for these euphonic occasions and writing "agent i consumes good l."

Varying language through inattention or simply for the sake of varying language is worse, of course, if the different terms actually designate different concepts. *Preference relation*, *utility*, and *utility function* are used interchangeably by some authors, but you should not do so. Choose your language in a way that preserves the important conceptual distinctions among such terms.

In subject areas in which terminology has not yet solidified, there may be even more choices than in well-established branches of the field. Do not, however, take this as a license to switch back and forth among several terms. Instead, seize the opportunity to steer the terminology in the right direction.

3.12 Name Concepts Carefully

When you introduce a definition, you need to find a term or phrase for it that suggests its content. If you use a multiword expression, do not worry too much about length; give priority to making sure that it describes the concept. In any case, you can always devise a shorter version. A good way of preparing us for the abbreviation is by placing in parentheses the part that you will subsequently omit, as in "A feasible allocation is (Pareto)-*efficient* if there is no other feasible allocation that all agents find at least as desirable and that at least one agent prefers." Later on, you can simply refer to *efficient allocations*. Of course, if you use several notions of efficiency, you will need to distinguish between them with different phrases. If you discuss only one type of efficiency, the shorter expression is unambiguous and slightly easier to use.

Actually, I do not see long expressions as much of a problem in a written text, as I explained earlier. In a seminar presentation, however, they may be troublesome. On those occasions, look for relatively short ones;

or, you can use the long but descriptive expression a few times—until you think your audience has absorbed the concept—then say, "From here on, I will only use the following shorter expression: . . . "

Designate assumptions by names that help keep the logical relations among them straight. *Strict monotonicity* should imply *monotonicity*, a condition that should, in turn, imply *weak monotonicity*. In an axiomatic study, axioms often come in various forms of different strength. Name them in a way that makes their hierarchy clear.

Keeping in mind that a given condition may have different interpretations depending on the context, choose neutral expressions that cover the various possible applications instead of phrases that are too intimately linked to the specific context of your paper. The requirement that an allocation rule should be monotonic with respect to each household's endowment—that is, the household's welfare should not decrease with an increase of its endowment—can be seen from the strategic viewpoint: violations of the requirement will make it profitable for the household to destroy some of the resources it controls. Alternatively, it may be motivated by fairness considerations: the household should derive some benefit from an increase in the resources it has earned. Therefore, instead of using phrases taken from game theory or from the theory of fair allocation, use a neutral expression such as *monotonicity*, (or *endowment monotonicity* if you also discuss monotonicities with respect to other parameters), letting your readers decide which interpretation they prefer.

3.13   Avoid Unnecessary Technical Jargon

Stick with plain language.

If a function is order preserving, do not say that it satisfies *order preservingness*; the name of the property is *order preservation*. The phrase *one-player coalition* for discussing cooperative games is awkward; you may have to speak separately of individual players and of coalitions (sets of two or more players). Also a theorem is proved by a person, not by a paper: "This result is established by Smith (1978)" is better than "This result is established in Smith (1978)." In common language, *preferring* means what in economese we often call *strictly preferring*; in our dialect we also have the dangerous phrase *weakly preferring*. It is dangerous because in standard English, having a weak preference for *A* over *B* means that we prefer *A* but that the intensity of the preference is mild; it does not mean that we may be indifferent to the choice between them. In most cases, you can rephrase references to economic ideas so as to avoid conflicts with common usage. When you feel you cannot, give priority to making an unambiguous statement. Of the three pairs "weakly prefers *versus* prefers," "prefers *versus* strictly prefers," "weakly prefers *versus* strictly prefers," the third one may thus be the best, even though it is the least grammatical. There is almost always, however, a grammatical way of expressing ourselves; in this example, we can speak of one object as being either at least as desirable as another one or preferable to it.

If a property has an adjectival form, you may have more options. For instance, it sounds a little better to say that "an allocation rule is *consistent*" than to say that "it satisfies *consistency*." A verbal form may be available too, giving you still additional freedom. I mentioned above allocation rules that are *order preserving*; but I suggest that you refer instead to rules that *preserve order*, using italics just as you would for the expression *order preserving* because it refers to a formally introduced property (if that is your typographical convention for these properties). So write "This section is devoted to an analysis of *order preservation*. Let φ be an allocation rule that *preserves order*."

One could argue that the special language we have developed in our trade is unavoidable and that our journals are not meant for the general public in any case. I agree with this to some extent, but I also believe that many specialists do not try hard enough to communicate their ideas in common language. The advice to avoid jargon is relevant to facilitate communication across other fields of economics. If you work, say, on the theory of implementation, limiting your use of technical language will gain you readers in other areas of economics—public finance or industrial organization, for example—areas to which this theory is relevant. This wider accessibility can only be beneficial to you and your subject.

3.14   Challenge Dominant But Inadequate Terminology and Usage

You are not obliged to use the language commonly employed by the writers who inspired your work if it is not felicitously chosen. You are allowed to improve on it, even if it used by prominent authors in the field, and by the profession at large. The same comment applies to notation.

For instance, the term *endowment* suggests—though admittedly it does not necessarily denote—resources that are owned initially (that is, prior to exchange and production). Thus the expression *initial endowment* is redundant. So just speak of the agents' endowments.[21] By the same token, why should the adjective *fair* be used to designate allocations that are both equitable and efficient, as it was in the early fairness literature? In common language, the term has no efficiency connotation at all. Refer instead to equitable and efficient allocations.

The condition of *independence of irrelevant alternatives* that appears in Nash's axiomatic derivation of what we now call the Nash solution is not well named. A phrase such as *contraction independence* might be preferable, because it is suggestive of the geometric operation that is being performed. Of course, it does not allow us to infer the exact nature of this operation; but neither does the standard expression. In fact, the latter is misleading, because it seems to prejudge the irrelevance of the deleted alternatives.[22] Readers will decide on their own whether these contractions are irrelevant.

Maskin-monotonicity is really an invariance condition: it states the invariance of the social choice under certain transformations of preferences—the term *monotonic* is appropriate to describe these transformations—and designating it by a phrase such as *invariance under monotonic transformations* might be clearer, especially for audiences not familiar with the implementation literature. (To some extent, our choice of language may indeed depend on how much our target audience knows about the subject.) In general, naming conditions after their authors is not as useful as naming them in a way that suggests their content. If the length of this alternate expression bothers you, what about *Maskin-invariance*?

The English language was not developed to label concepts of mathematics or economics; but the closer the fit between the concept you are naming and the common meaning of the term, the better. For most conditions, it is true, you probably won't find a short phrase that unambiguously describes your hypotheses and conclusions. Strive for the right balance between compactness and precision.

---

21. Besides, if you have to consider changes in the endowment of a player—for instance, to find out whether the owner of two left gloves may gain by throwing away one of them prior to entering the market—you will be forced to make the agent go from the pleonastic "initial initial endowments" to the oxymoronic "final initial endowments." Whatever benefit is derived from this clever move will be more than canceled out by the embarrassment of using bad English.

22. A convincing case can be made that the condition covers situations in which the deleted alternatives are not irrelevant and in which, therefore, the solution outcome should not be required to stay the same.

If you introduce a new phrase, indicate the names that others have used for the condition. Here too footnotes are handy.

3.15   Use Technical Terms Correctly

Mathematical terms have precise meanings, and you should respect this language. Do not use the term *vector* unless you will perform vector space operations. If you have in mind a collection of objects taken from some set, the appropriate terms are *lists*, *ordered lists*, or *profiles*.

The notation $(R_1, \ldots, R_n)$ refers to an ordered list of preference relations (or a preference profile), not to a vector of preference relations: you will probably not compute $(R_1 + R_2)/2$. On the other hand, it is often appropriate to present a list $(s_1, \ldots, s_n)$ of strategies as a strategy *vector*. In a game form designed to implement a solution to a public goods problem, an agent's strategy may be a public good level, and the outcome function may select the average of the announced levels. Consumption bundles are usually vectors. You often compute averages of bundles or multiply them by two.

Do not confuse functions with the values they take. If $f : \mathbb{R} \to \mathbb{R}$ is a function, $f(x)$ is the value the function takes when its argument is x. So $f(x)$ cannot be differentiable, or concave, and so on. These are properties of f and not of its values. Designate the function simply by f [which is better than $f(\cdot)$]. Similarly, $u_i(x_i)$ is not agent i's utility function; u_i is. Conversely, if you choose u_i to denote agent i's utility function, do not also use u_i to denote the particular value this function takes for a certain choice of its argument.

If F is a solution to a class of bargaining problems (a mapping defined on a domain of problems that associates with each problem in the domain a payoff vector that is feasible for the problem), and S is a problem in its domain of definition, $F(S)$ is no longer a solution but something like a *solution outcome*, or the *solution outcome of S*. Alternatively, you can call F a *solution concept* and refer to $F(S)$ as the *solution of S*.

3.16   Clean Up Your Text

Go over your paper word by word and ask yourself whether each one is the best you can use and whether it fits with its neighbors. Ask whether you need it at all. You will find that many words can be deleted with no loss of meaning or clarity. The goal is not to shorten your paper, however, but to make it cleaner.

Here are some illustrations of ways to lighten your prose. Instead of speaking of "the agents in the economy," refer to them as "the agents." If consumers are your only agents, do not write that "consumers' preferences are assumed to be convex." In such a case, preferences can only be consumers' preferences. "Preferences are assumed to be convex" is better. Better still—convexity being only one of the many assumptions that you make in specifying your model—simplify the sentence to "preferences are convex." Applying the same idea to firms, replace "The technologies of the firms in the economy are assumed to be convex" with "Technologies are convex." (Firms are in the economy; technologies are the technologies of the firms; convexity is a property of technologies that you are assuming.) Are you reluctant to delete "are assumed" from "Preferences are assumed to be convex"? Then, why did you write "The horizon is finite," as opposed to "The horizon is assumed to be finite"? Checking your whole text will demonstrate that you distributed the *is/are assumed* pairs randomly. I am confident that you can delete most of them.

Here are a few other examples of the sort of clean-up operations I recommend. The expressions in the left-hand column are not as smooth and clean as those in the right-hand column:

Therefore we have that $a > b$. (In this sentence, the inequality sign is read as a verb.)	Therefore we have $a > b$. (Here, the inequality sign is read as an adjective in the comparative form.)
Therefore we have $a > b$.	Therefore $a > b$. (Here, once again, the inequality sign is read as a verb.)
Either $a > b$ or $a' > b'$ holds.	Either $a > b$ or $a' > b'$.
If A holds, it must be that $x \geq y$.	If A, then $x \geq y$." (Every implication, if correct, is a "must.")
If the equality $a = b$ holds,	If $a = b$,
Using the fact that $a > b$,	Since $a > b$,
A function is monotone if it is such that for all $x, y \ldots$	A function is monotone if for all $x, y \ldots$
Providing an explanation,	Explaining
Minimization exercises	Minimizations
Lexicographic operations	Lexicographic minimizations or lexicographic maximizations (depending upon which it is)

The cardinality of the set of objects is smaller than n	The number of objects is smaller than n
A characterization result	A characterization
The condition was first introduced by Smith	Smith introduced the condition
The set of Nash equilibria is a nonempty set.	Nash equilibrium exists.
Because of the differentiability property of cost functions	Since cost functions are differentiable
In this paper, we show	We show

If English is not your first language, ask for assistance. To weed out of your text its gallicisms, nipponisms, sinocisms, and so on, get help from a native gardener.

4   Models

In this section, I discuss how to present your model and convey the intuition that led to your main results, introduce the various assumptions under which you conduct your analysis, and state your results.

4.1   Understand the Role of Models

Your model is a tool, not reality. You specified it in order to study a phenomenon of interest. You should, therefore, not get carried away when drawing conclusions about the real world from your results. On the other hand, you do not have to defend the model as an accurate and complete representation of the world. We know it is not. It only needs to include all the essential elements for describing and studying the target problem.

4.2   Introduce Your Model by Moving from Infrastructure to Superstructure

In specifying an economy, introduce and describe each actor category separately before bringing them together. For instance, in a general equilibrium problem, describe consumers first—their endowments, their preferences, and what they know. Next, introduce the producers and specify technologies. Then bring all these actors together to compose the economy. Up to this point, economics has played no role in the model; preferences belong to the realm of psychology and are given to you by the psychologist; technologies have to do with engineering and come from the engineer.

Once all the actors are in place, you can define the notion of an allocation and explain what it means for an allocation to be feasible. Note that the material balances you specify for this definition still have nothing to do with economic institutions. The economic analysis proper begins only when you start allocating resources by, say, quoting prices and asking consumers to maximize preferences in budget sets and producers to maximize profits subject to technological constraints.

The idea here is to keep separate concepts separate and to ensure that this separation is reflected in the language you use. For example, the hypothesis on indifference curves, that they can all be obtained from any one of them by arbitrary translations parallel to the horizontal axis, implies the absence of income effects at interior points. But this property is meaningful only if you have already defined Walrasian notions of prices and incomes. Therefore, saying that preferences are quasi-linear is better than saying that they exhibit no income effects, because the former does not prejudge your choice of economic institutions. Quasi-linearity does imply the absence of income effects, but it is also useful in certain contexts in which Walrasian notions play no role. For instance, you may be interested in allocating resources by applying the solution concepts developed in the theory of games with transferable utility; quasi-linearity of preferences will let you do that.

4.3   Avoid Long Sentences

A good way to prevent ambiguities is to write mostly one-clause sentences. If English is not your native language, doing so will also greatly help you avoid grammatical errors. Finally, limiting yourself to such sentences will force you to put them down in logical sequences. Here is an illustration of the idea:

Let (S, h) be a game form. Let $\mathcal{R}^n$ be a class of admissible profiles of preference relations over Z. Given $R \in \mathcal{R}^n$, the triple (S, h, R) is a *game*. A *Nash equilibrium of* (S, h, R) is a point $s \in S$ such that for all $i \in N$ and all $s_i' \in S_i$, we have $h_i(s) R_i h_i(s_i', s_{-i})$. If $s \in S$ is an equilibrium, $h(s) \in Z$ is the corresponding *equilibrium outcome*. Let $E(S, h, R) \subseteq Z$ denote the set of equilibrium outcomes of the game (S, h, R). *The game* *form (S, h) implements the correspondence $\varphi: \mathcal{R}^n \to Z$ if for all preference profiles $R \in \mathcal{R}^n$, we have $E(S, h, R) = \varphi(R)$.*

You may think that your chance for a Nobel prize in literature will not be much improved by this staccato style. Yet I could name several grammatically impaired writers, who hardly ever used subordinate or relative clauses and yet who still got to make the trip to Stockholm! If you do not like this kind of choppy writing, reconnect some of your shortest sentences in your very last draft. But you do not have to. Your text will acquire rhythm and even a certain formal elegance. So, even from the viewpoint of aesthetics, you may gain.

By the same token, break your text into paragraphs of reasonable length, keeping in mind that too much of a good thing is a bad thing: a sequence of one-sentence paragraphs is not pleasant to read. But there is no rule about how long a paragraph should be. Identify the most natural places for giving your reader a slightly longer pause. Let logic dictate or suggest where the divisions should be.

4.4   Redundancy Is Useful, But Don't Overdo It

Yes, a certain amount of redundancy in your explanations *is* useful, but do not overdo it.[23]

For instance, giving an informal description of the main steps of a proof, or maybe simply restating before presenting a proof that it holds only because a certain restriction on preferences is imposed—a point that you have developed in a preceding section—is not strictly necessary. But it might be quite helpful. The principle here is the same as the one underlying the notion of defensive driving; that is, driving under the assumption that other drivers will make mistakes. *Defensive writing* proceeds under the assumption that a reader may be distracted at a critical moment. You may have properly stated the important restriction without which your result does not hold. But if you did not emphasize it sufficiently and a reader is confused, it does not help you to know that the reader could have understood it by paying closer attention. (Just as knowing that your accident was the other driver's fault does not help you recover from your injuries.) Such additional explanations should not, however, appear within the proof itself but should precede it, so

---

23. I mean that it is sometimes helpful to explain an argument in several different ways; but you should not explain the same things in too many different ways. (You must agree, this footnote is redundant.)

as to prepare us for it. The proof itself should be as concise as you can make it without hampering readability.

Another circumstance under which redundancy is not only acceptable but probably desirable is in facilitating transitions from one section to the next. Transitions should make sense to readers even if they do not read the section heading. Thus you may have to begin each section with a sentence that essentially repeats the heading, which, unlike the headings of this essay (which I wrote as injunctions), is often not a complete sentence. Often you can simply convert the heading into a sentence; at other times you will have to express its content in a slightly different way.

When stating a difficult definition, assist us by giving an informal explanation in addition to the formal statement. Here, too, such an explanation should come before the formal statement, to prepare readers for it and save them from frustration.[24] It is annoying to spend time struggling to understand a complicated concept when it is first given, only to discover that two paragraphs down the author was willing to help after all.

The same comment applies to figures. If you provided a figure to illustrate a proof, thank you very much, but why didn't you say so ahead of time, so that readers can identify on it the variables as you introduced them and use it to follow your argument? Warning us that one exists is especially important because the constraints of typesetting make it hard to control a figure's exact placement in text and a figure illustrating a proof may very well appear on the page following the proof instead of next to the proof.

4.5   Don't Be Shy About Explaining Very Simple Things

To ensure that everything is clear to everyone, you may sometimes have to take time and space to explain things that seem very simple to you. This is especially true in a seminar, as you will not have time to explain the complicated issues in any detail, and especially at the beginning. Indeed, if you lose your audience then you may have a hard time getting it back.

---

24. Did you notice that I sometimes refer to *the reader*, sometimes to *your reader* (singular), sometimes to *your readers* (plural), and sometimes to *us*, your readers? This is an example of an inconsistency of style that should be avoided. So should *should be avoided*. As I have throughout addressed you, my reader, I should have written *that you should avoid*. I return to the issue of consistency of style in subsection 5.7.

After stating an *if* and *only if* theorem, do not refer to the "if part" and the "only if" part. Similarly, do not refer to the "sufficiency part" and the "necessity part" of a theorem stating that it is necessary and sufficient that A holds for B to be true. Certainly do not refer to the "necessity part" after having stated your theorem as an *if and only if* theorem. Though this language seems standard enough, most people will not be sure which direction you mean or will know it only by expending energy better spent on other things. I have even seen some of the greatest economists confused about this distinction; in my personal pantheon, they are people whose approach to economics cannot be described as "literary." Avoid the problem by just restating the result in each direction as you discuss it.

Similarly, would you believe that most of your professors really do not know what a marginal rate of substitution is? But it's true! To most of us, a sentence such as "Agent 1's marginal rate of substitution at z_0 is greater than agent 2's" only means that the two agents' indifference curves through z_0 have different slopes at z_0. We can only hope that it will be clear which one of them is steeper when we really need to know. Of course, we would never admit confusion by asking publicly, and I certainly would never put such a confession in writing for fear of being forever shunned by my colleagues. To prevent this situation, compare the agents' marginal rates of substitution of good 2 for good 1 at the point z_0; even better, simply talk about their indifference curves being more or less steep at z_0.

It is a great unsolved mystery of neuroscience why someone can prove the fanciest theorems in the most abstract spaces and yet have trouble with some very elementary operations. Remember that. After all, haven't you called your relatives in England at 3 A.M. their time after carefully calculating that it would be 3 P.M.? You might have failed in such a trivial calculation but brilliantly passed exams that tested much more of your intellect.

4.6 *Beware the Apparent Simplicity of Numerical Examples*

People often think that numerical examples provide easy introductions to complicated proofs. But this is true only when examples are well chosen. A general algebraic expression, in fact, is often a better way to help readers see the logic of an argument. If, to fix ideas, you choose $x_1 = 1$ and $x_2 = 8$, the number 9 will refer to the sum $x_1 + x_2$; but it might be useful to remember how it arose and to write "$1 + 8$" instead, or "9 $(=1+8)$." The expression $x_1 + x_2$ may be preferable. In a three-player game, write the number of coalitions as $2^3 - 1$; we do not care whether that number is equal to 7. If three mutually exclusive events occur with probabilities 1/2, 1/3, and 1/6, write these probabilities as 3/6, 2/6, and 1/6, or, better still, as $\frac{3}{6}$, $\frac{2}{6}$, and $\frac{1}{6}$. Simplifying the fractions will make it less easy for readers to see that you are applying Bayes's law.

Moreover, if you use numerical examples instead of algebraic notation, you may lose track of units of measurement, making it harder to check the correctness of expressions. The efficiency condition in a public-good economy in which the public good is produced by means of a one-to-one technology (one unit of the input yielding one unit of the output) is that the sum across agents of their marginal rates of substitution of the private good for the public good at their respective bundles is equal to one. But it is more informative to write that this sum is equal to the marginal rate of transformation at the corresponding production point (a rate that happens to be equal to one, again measured in "private good over public good"). Remember that college physics homework in which you discovered a mistake in an equation by noting that temperature appeared with different exponents on each side? If, instead, you had given a numerical value to the temperature, you would never have noticed. The same principle applies here.

When you vary a parameter, as a result of which agent 1's income increases from 5 to 7 and agent 2's income decreases from 8 to 5, it will soon be difficult to remember which figures are the initial incomes, which are the final incomes, and whose income is 5 and when. If you choose your notation well—for instance by calling the incomes I_1 and I_2 before the change and I_1' and I_2' after the change—readers cannot be confused. That is what you should do, even if you do not manipulate the symbols further.

If you insist on using numbers, however, choose figures that, no matter what operation you perform on them, do not turn them into monsters. If you will divide x_1 by 2, choose x_1 even; if you will take its square root, do not choose $x_1 = 10$.

Actually, I take this back. It depends: if the incomes are 5 and 7 initially, and they are cut in half, they will be 5/2 and 7/2 after the change and the fractions will make it easier to remember that they are the new ones. If they were even you would be tempted to perform the division to get integers; here again, it would be hard to tell the new incomes from the old ones.

In filling a payoff matrix, take all payoffs to be integers between 0 and 9 and you will not have to separate them by commas. In each cell you can also place the payoff of the row player slightly higher than that of the column player.

More useful than numerical examples are examples with a small number of agents, a small number of goods, and no production. You save on subscripts, you can use an Edgeworth box, and your proof can appeal to the intermediate value theorem instead of to a general fixed-point theorem.

By the same token, general arguments are sometimes easier to understand than their applications to particular situations. It is more transparent why a competitive equilibrium is Pareto efficient when the proof is presented in the general case than, say, for a Cobb-Douglas economy. There is indeed little to be learned from the calculations for a special case.

Similarly, illustrating a general phenomenon with a perhaps incompletely specified geometric example is more informative than using a complete argument based on a particular numerical example. This is because it may not be obvious which features of the numerical example are essential to the phenomenon. To prove that in an Edgeworth box economy there could be several Walrasian equilibria, it suffices to use an example in which preferences are suggested by means of a few indifference curves for each of the two agents. Of course, a few indifference curves do not constitute a preference map; and you have to rely on your readers' experience with such maps to help them mentally complete your figure—or convince themselves that completion is possible. The alternative is to give entire maps, in most cases this will require providing explicit numerical representations for them. These representations will often be quite complicated. Although they will prove your point beyond doubt, I strongly believe that they will hamper understanding of the circumstances under which multiple equilibria occur.

If in a proof you can reach the desired conclusion by choosing some parameter α arbitrarily in the interval $[0, 1]$, write so as to make this clear: "Let $\alpha \in [0, 1]$" is better than "Let $\alpha = 1/2$," which might lead us to believe that there is something special about $1/2$. If the calculations are easier with $1/2$, write "Let $\alpha \in [0, 1]$, say $\alpha = 1/2$."

4.7   If You Name Your Agents, Do So in a Helpful Way

If you think numbering your agents from 1 to 4 is too dry when describing an example, try real names. But choose them carefully so readers can easily remember who is who. Naming them Bob and Carol, Ted and

Alice will be cute but may be counterproductive. Ted in particular does not belong in the group because he prevents you from ordering your four consumers by consecutive letters of the alphabet: Alice and Bob, Carol and Det are your four consumers. In honor of a favorite writer, I have often wanted to call agents 1 and 2 Qfwfq and Xlthlx. But which is easier to keep track of: agent 1 is endowed with good 1 and agent 2 is endowed with good 2, or Qfwfq is endowed with apples, and Xlthlx is endowed with oranges?

By the way, in a seminar avoid cultural references that are obscure to too many in your audience, but do not, by all means, avoid such references altogether. Sometimes it will not be easy to decide whether listeners will understand. Do you think, for example, that I should have resisted the temptation to quote *"Erreur, tu n'es pas un mal"* to prevent readers who do not know French from feeling excluded—thereby depriving the rest of us of this beautiful maxim? What is the correct criterion of social-choice theory here?[25]

4.8 Use One Enumeration for Each Object Category

Number each category of objects, definitions, propositions, theorems, and so on separately. Some authors use a single list for all numbered items: Definition 15, which is the tenth definition, is followed by Theorem 16, which is the third theorem; Theorem 16 is followed by Corollary 17, which is the only corollary and so on. Separate numbering is preferable, as it clarifies the organization of a paper. If you have two main sections, with one theorem in each, label the theorems Theorem 1 and Theorem 2. A single list does facilitate retrieving a needed item, but this benefit is too small. Bringing out the structure of your paper is more important. I checked with a musicologist friend of mine: Beethoven's Symphony No. 9 is his ninth symphony, not his third.[26]

---

25. I referred once to Bob and Carol and Ted and Alice in a seminar in which I discussed matching theory, and someone in the audience commented that I was showing my age. I was unfortunately not quick enough—showing my age once again—to reply that by understanding that I was showing my age, and remarking on it, he was showing his. He was right though. I recently asked the students in my graduate class whether they understood the allusion. Not one of them did. And yet, *Bob & Carol & Ted & Alice* (it's a movie) came out only yesterday (thirty-one years ago, to be precise). From now on, I will use this example only when lecturing in retirement homes.

26. For long documents such as books, adding to the label of a theorem the page number on which it is stated might be useful: Theorem 3.123 would designate the third theorem of the chapter, which appears on page 123. The more common editorial convention, however, is to add a cross-reference when a theorem is discussed later in the book (for example, *see p. 123*).

4.9   State Assumptions in Order of Decreasing Plausibility or Generality

When introducing your assumptions, start with the most natural ones and proceed to those that are increasingly restrictive and decreasingly plausible. You should always postpone as long as possible the moment when a reader may not be entirely comfortable with some aspects of your argument. When you refer to the assumptions again, of course, use the same order, for the same reasons. Sometimes, however, there is no unique natural order and you will have to make a choice. Once your choice is made, stick with it throughout the paper.

For utility functions, do not write

$A1$: u_i is strictly concave,

$A2$: u_i is bounded,

$A3$: u_i is continuous.

Instead (and here I do not attempt to give names to the conditions), write

$A1$: u_i is continuous,

$A2$: u_i is bounded,

$A3$: u_i is strictly concave.

An enumeration should be logical: proceeding from small to large, easy to difficult, particular to general, and so on; for example, "All economic agents respond to incentives: paper boys, corner grocers, companies quoted on the stock exchange, and multinational corporations."

4.10   Group Assumptions by Category

Introduce your assumptions in related groups.

For a general equilibrium model,

$A1$–$A5$ pertain to consumers,

$B1$–$B6$ pertain to firms.

For a game,

$A1$–$A3$ pertain to the structure of the game,

$B1$–$B2$ pertain to the behavior of the players.

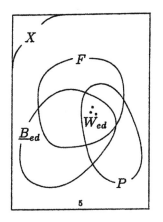

Figure 1.6
How to Indicate Logical Relationships Between Concepts. Key: X is the feasible set, P the set of Pareto-efficient allocations, F the set of envy-free allocation, $\underline{B}_{ed}$ the set of allocations meeting the equal division lower bound, W_{ed} the set of equal income Walrasian allocations. The set of feasible allocations is so large in relation to the set of Pareto-efficient allocations that its bubble does not even fit in the page. There are continua of Pareto-efficient allocations and of envy-free allocations but typically a finite number of equal-division Walrasian allocations. A small tip: breaking the boundary of a bubble to make room for its label is the best way to make the labeling unambiguous.

4.11 Figure Out and Indicate Logical Relations among Assumptions and Groups of Assumptions

Find out how your conditions are logically related. If these relations are complex, present them in the form of diagrams. In a seminar, show diagrams of implications even if relations among them are not complex. Venn diagrams (figure 1.6), with each bubble symbolizing the set of objects satisfying one of the conditions, are the most effective.

If you represent the bubbles associated with Conditions A and B as partially overlapping, it is because neither one implies the other, which you know from having identified

1. At least one object satisfying A but not B,
2. At least one object satisfying B but not A,
3. At least one object satisfying both.

You can also use a diagram of arrows (figure 1.7), each indicating an implication, and crossed arrows, each indicating a lack of implication. But an advantage of Venn diagrams is that by drawing bubbles of

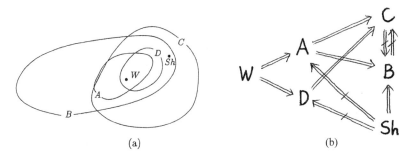

(a)   (b)

Figure 1.7
Venn Diagrams Convey Much More Information Than Arrows. The two diagrams seem
to convey the same information about logical relations, but the Venn diagram (a) allows
you to show that "few" objects satisfy condition A but not condition C, whereas many
satisfy condition B but not condition A. It also allows you to place individual objects,
such as the Walrasian rule or the Shapley value, in the appropriate places. I made this
diagram of arrows (b) deliberately messy to strengthen my claim that Venn diagrams are
better than diagrams of arrows, but even if I were fair, bubbles would look better.

appropriate size you can convey additional information about the relative strengths of conditions. If A is much stronger than B, draw a much
smaller bubble for A. If you establish under Condition B a conclusion
that was derived under A in earlier literature, you need to give readers
a sense of how significant the weakening is. Of course, how restrictive A
is in relation to B is a subjective judgment; but in this case, subjectivity
is unavoidable.

A second advantage of Venn diagrams is that they make it easy to
indicate the joint implications of several conditions. If A and B together
imply C, the two bubbles representing them intersect within the bubble
representing C. If you use an arrow diagram, you would have to merge
two arrows emanating from A and B and point the merged arrow at C.
You would end up with a big mess.

If you do not link two conditions when using arrows, you are indicating that you do not know how they are related or that it is not important
to know. This option does not exist with Venn diagrams. Therefore, a
disadvantage of these diagrams is that in order not to be misleading,
you need to figure out all the logical relations between your conditions.
But this disadvantage is an advantage.[27] Do the work; you will never
regret it.

---

27. An effective way to proceed is to figure out all the illogical relations; then those
remaining are the logical relations.

A final advantage of Venn diagrams is that you can sometimes draw the bubbles in a way that suggests some of the structure of the sets they represent: if the set is convex, draw a convex bubble; if it is defined by a system of linear inequalities, give it a polygonal boundary; if it is a lattice, draw it as a diamond, and so on.

4.12 Make Sure There Are Objects Satisfying All Your Assumptions

For each theorem, you should point to at least one object satisfying all your assumptions. After stating that you will consider economies satisfying Assumptions 1–10, give an example that does so. (Try Cobb-Douglas; it will probably work.) If the class of objects satisfying your assumptions is empty, any statement you will make about these objects will be mathematically correct but of limited usefulness.

4.13 Use a Common Format for Formal Statements of Results and Similar Parts of Proofs

If you have several results that are variants of each other, present them in the same format so as to make their relations to each other immediately apparent. If you first state

THEOREM 1   If A, B, and C, then D and E.

Do not write your next theorem, which differs from Theorem 1 in that C is replaced by C' and E is replaced by $\tilde{E}$, as

THEOREM 2   Suppose A and B. In addition, consider the class of economies satisfying C'. Then D. Also, $\tilde{E}$ holds.

Instead, use a paralell format.[28]

THEOREM 2   If A, B, and C', then D and $\tilde{E}$.

How Theorems 1 and 2 relate to each other will then be obvious, and readers will discover it by simply scanning them. Choosing different

---

28. My incorrect spelling of *paralell* (Darn, I did it again!) is an unfortunate consequence of having finally mastered that of A. Mas-Colell's name (the name for which, in my estimation, the ratio of incorrect to correct spellings is the highest in the profession). Do spell names correctly! Dupont does not want to be confused with Dupond any more than Schultze identifies with Schulze. Hernandez and Fernandez are two different people. Thompson is very attached to his p, and I know for a fact that Thomson has no desire for one.

formats for the theorems would force readers to actually read the entire statements and make, hypothesis by hypothesis and conclusion by conclusion, the comparisons needed for a good understanding of their relationship. In some cases, it will be possible to present the two theorems as parts 1 and 2 of a single theorem.[29] Physical proximity and a common format are two important ways to facilitate readers' task.

Similarly, a proof may consist of several parts having identical or almost identical structures. Present them in a way that brings out this similarity. Instead of writing out Case 1 and Case 2 separately, write Case 1 first, and work on it until it is in perfect shape; then copy and paste it and make the adjustments necessary to cover Case 2. The similarities of phrasing and format will unambiguously signal readers that if they understand Case 1, they can skip Case 2; or that if they do read Case 2, they will incur minimal marginal costs.

Should you be concerned about the repetitive nature of your text if you write in this way? Not at all. Revealing the structure of an argument helps readers understand and saves time and effort.

To ensure that the various parts of a paper that should be are formatted or styled in a similar fashion, go over the whole paper reading only those parts. Read all the theorems and only them, and compare their statements. If Theorem 1 is "Under Assumptions 1–5, a Nash equilibrium exists," Theorem 2 should not be "Under Assumptions 1–4 and 6, there is at least one Nash equilibrium," but "Under Assumptions 1–4 and 6, a Nash equilibrium exists." Or perhaps it is the wording of Theorem 1 that you should change to "Under Assumptions 1–5, there is at least one Nash equilibrium."

Compare the formats and styles of your assumptions as well, making sure that all come from the same mold. Repeat the operation for axioms, figure legends, remarks, and so on. These comparisons will not only ensure consistency of presentation but may also show you that what you thought were equivalent formulations are in fact not quite the same. You will discover that one is slightly better than the other, or that one that is better still could be obtained by combining the best features of each. The two theorems I just gave as examples sound the same; but the phrasing "There is at least one Nash equilibrium" prepares us a little better than "A Nash equilibrium exists" for the possibility that

---

29. Capitalize the word *theorem* when it refers to a specific theorem (as in Theorem 1 above) but not in a sentence such as "Capitalize the word *theorem* when ..." The same rule applies to propositions, sections, figures, and so on.

there might be several equilibria. You should, therefore, choose the first phrase if multiplicity of equilibria will be important in later parts of your paper.

Another exercise that greatly helps to eliminate errors and improve the exposition of your work is to prepare several versions of a paper: perhaps one version for the technical journal you intend to submit it to and a more expository version for a seminar or lecture. Writing each version will give you ideas for improving the other. Often some of the simplifications that made the expository version easier to understand will help make the technical version more transparent. I have often discovered that some ways of streamlining a technical paper to better convey my idea to an unspecialized audience (say, in a general departmental seminar) are also effective with an audience of those very familiar with the subject (for example, a graduate class or a specialized conference). I am sure that even readers who understand your complicated concepts or proofs will prefer a simpler presentation of them.

5   Theorems and Proofs

Having introduced notation, language, and model, you can proceed to theorems and write the proofs.

5.1   *Choose the Right Mixture of Words and Mathematics in Proofs*

A proof written entirely in English is often not precise enough and is too long. A proof written entirely in mathematics is impossible to understand—unless, of course, you are a digital computer. Modern estimation techniques have shown that a proof's optimal ratio of mathematics to English lies between 52 and 63.5 percent. Pick the point on that interval that is right for you and stick with it (see figure 1.8).

The theorems themselves, however, should be stated in the simplest English possible. The reader who wants to know more than the usually informal description of the results given in the introduction may be able to spare only few more minutes for reading the paper. Just reading theorems that are simply and clearly written will give such a reader a much more precise understanding of your contribution at a very small cost. Admittedly, it is sometimes difficult to achieve such readability—for technical papers it is probably impossible. But try. If you are successful, even skimmers and skippers will be induced to stay with your work a little longer.

(a)

All I have to do is deduce, from what I know of you, the way your mind works. Are you the kind of man who would put the poison into his own glass, or into the glass of his enemy? [...] Now a great fool [...] would place the a wine in front of his own goblet, because he would know that only another great fool would reach first for what he was given. I am clearly not a great fool, so I will clearly not reach for your wine [...] We have now decided the poisoned cup is most likely in front of you. But the poison is powder made from iocane and iocane comes only from Australia and Australia, as everyone knows, is peopled with criminals and criminals are used to having people not trust them, and I don't trust you, which means that I can clearly not choose the wine in front of you [...] But again, you must have suspected I knew the origins of iocane, so you would have known I knew about the criminals and criminal behavior, and therefore I can clearly not choose the wine in front of me [...] You have beaten my Turk, which means you are exceptionally strong, and exceptionally strong men are convinced that they are too powerful ever to die, too powerful even for iocane powder, so you could have put it in your own cup, trusting on your strength to save you; thus I can clearly not choose the wine in front of you [...] But you also bested my Spaniard, which means that you must have studied, because he studied many years for his excellence, and if you can study, you are clearly more than simply strong; you are aware of how mortal we all are, and you do not wish to die, so you would have kept the poison as far from yourself as possible; therefore I can clearly not choose the wine in front of me.

(b)

Proof: This follows from the inclusion $\varphi \subseteq P$, Part (i) of Proposition 1, and Lemma 1 applied to φ.

(c)

Figure 1.8
The Ratio of Mathematics to English in a Proof Should Be in the Right Interval. The proof in (a) has too much math. Because of its high density of mathematical symbols, it is virtually impossible to understand. (I can only make out that it states the existence of ducks having certain properties.) (b) This game-theoretic proof has too much English; it is not precise enough and is too long. Not surprisingly, two paragraphs down, the character who produced it is dead. (He has to choose one of two cups of wine and drink from it. His opponent, who told him that he has poisoned one of them, will drink from the other). (c) This proof is just right, said Goldilocks, and that is the one she read. It is indeed pleasantly short and clean. Wouldn't you like to know what theorem it proves? (None, it turns out. I made it up.)

5.2 Divide Proofs into Clearly Identified Steps or Cases

Divide your proofs into clearly identified, meaningful units. Indent and double indent to indicate structure. Name and number units (for example, Step 1, Step 2, Case 1, Subcase 1a, Subcase 1b, Claim 1, etc.). If the proof is long and complex, give each step, case, or claim a title indicating its content. Make sure that we know whether this title is a statement you will prove or an obvious conclusion that readers should reach on their own, as in steps 1 and 2 below:

Step 1. The domain of the correspondence φ is compact. To prove this, we will establish two claims:

Claim 1. The domain is bounded. To see this . . .

Claim 2. The domain is closed. This follows from Lemma 1.

Step 2. The correspondence φ is upper semicontinuous.

If the claims are conceptual units of independent interest—certainly if they are used in other parts of the paper—as opposed to claims pertaining to a list of similar cases that have to be checked in turn, call them *lemmas* (or *lemmata*, the Greek plural; not *lemmatas*, unless you really have lots of them!) and present them separately.

If a proof is long, you may have to number some of the statements it is composed of and to refer to them by these numbers. Unfortunately, numbering quickly increases the complexity of the proof (I mean, how complex it looks). If you do this, number only the essential statements. If, for instance, you end a sentence by establishing a statement used as a hypothesis in your next sentence and if the statement is not used elsewhere, do not number it.

In a proof by contradiction, you do not have to contradict twice. For instance, to show that there is no object satisfying Conditions 1 and 2, you may start with "Let O be an object satisfying Conditions 1 and 2" and end by establishing that O could not satisfy Condition 2 after all. If in reaching this conclusion you never use the fact that O satisfies Condition 2, you should, instead, start with "Let O be an object satisfying Condition 1" and go on to show, as before, that O cannot satisfy Condition 2.

5.3   Gather in Front of a Conclusion All the Conditions Needed to Reach It

Hypotheses should come first and be written together. Do not distribute them on both sides of the conclusion, as in "If A and B, then D since C" or "If A and B, then D. This is because C." Instead, write "If A, B, and C, then D."

Especially for long statements, it helps to visually separate the hypotheses from the conclusions by *then, we have, it follows that*, or a similar phrase. If you write "Since A, B, C, and D," readers will not be sure whether you mean "Since A, then B, C, and D," or "Since A and B, then C and D," even though grammar dictates that the former is correct. Nonetheless, they won't figure this out until they reach the end of the sentence. It is better to make it clear *as it happens* that you are switching from hypotheses to conclusions.

Using a few English words to separate complicated expressions makes it easier to see where each one starts and ends. Writing "For all $i \in N$, $x_i R_i x_i'$" is no problem because the sentence is short and both parts are simple and familiar. But consider: "For all $h = (h_1^*, h_2^*, \ldots, h_K^*)$, $\bar{\pi}(h) = (\pi_1(h_1^*), \pi_2(h_2^*), \ldots, \pi_K(h_K^*))$." To make it easier to read, write "For all $h = (h_1^*, h_2^*, \ldots, h_K^*)$, we have $\bar{\pi}(h) = (\pi_1(h_1^*), \pi_2(h_2^*), \ldots, \pi_K(h_K^*))$" or display the second part—especially if it is a meaningful expression readers will encounter again—and dispense with "we have." You would write "For all $h = (h_1^*, h_2^*, \ldots, h_K^*)$,

$$\bar{\pi}(h) = (\pi_1(h_1^*), \pi_2(h_2^*), \ldots, \pi_K(h_K^*)).\text{"}$$

Mathematical statements usually look better when all the quantifications appear together, preferably at the beginning, instead of being distributed on both sides of the predicate. For instance, instead of "For all $x \in X$, we have $x_i > y_i$ for all $i \in N$," write "For all $x \in X$ and all $i \in N$, we have $x_i > y_i$." By the way, this example illustrates a possible conflict between two of my recommendations. If you took my advice to separate mathematical expressions by English words, you might change "for all $h = (h_1^*, h_2^*, \ldots, h_K^*)$, $\bar{\pi}(h) = (\pi_1(h_1^*), \pi_2(h_2^*), \ldots, \pi_K(h_K^*))$" to "for all $h = (h_1^*, h_2^*, \ldots, h_K^*)$, we have $\bar{\pi}(h) = (\pi_1(h_1^*), \pi_2(h_2^*), \ldots, \pi_K(h_K^*))$"; but the formulation "$\bar{\pi}(h) = (\pi_1(h_1^*), \pi_2(h_2^*), \ldots, \pi_K(h_K^*))$ for all $h = (h_1^*, h_2^*, \ldots, h_K^*)$," in which the quantification occurs *after* the equality, also achieves the desired separation and is slightly shorter.

5.4 *Pay Special Attention to Quantifications*

Quantifications deserve special care. Let's look first at the case of multiple quantifications in which the same variable appears twice. Suppose that an economy is defined as a pair consisting of a preference profile R chosen in the domain $\mathcal{R}^N$ and a social endowment Ω chosen from $\mathbb{R}_+^\ell$, and that you are making a statement about all pairs of economies that differ only in their social endowments. Let $\mathcal{E} \equiv \mathcal{R}^N \times \mathbb{R}_+^\ell$ designate the class of economies you are considering. Do not then write "For all (R, Ω),

$(R, \Omega') \in \mathcal{E}$," because the variable R appears with a universal quantification twice. You have to write "For all $(R, \Omega) \in \mathcal{E}$ and all $\Omega' \in \mathbb{R}_+^\ell$" or "For all (R, Ω) and $(R', \Omega') \in \mathcal{E}$ such that $R = R'$." If $\mathcal{E}$ is not the Cartesian product of a domain of preference relations and a domain of social endowments, you should choose a formulation of the second type.

Next, if a certain quantification applies to only one of two successive statements, order them so as to make the scope of the quantification clear. "There exists a such that for all i, $P(a, i)$ and $Q(a)$" is not as good as "There exists a such that $Q(a)$ and for all i, $P(a, i)$," because the quantification over i is only relevant to statement P. For statements as simple as the one I just wrote it may not matter much, but if both P and Q were complicated expressions with multiple variables it could take some time to discover that i does not appear in Q.

If, starting from some list of objects $(O_1, \ldots, O_n)$, you want to say that one of them is equal to A, write "there exists $i \in N$ such that $O_i = A$," not "there exists O_i such that $O_i = A$." As the proof continues, you probably will have to refer to the particular i you just identified.

Finally, an issue of style: If you use descriptive names when listing objects in an enumeration to remind us of what they are, be consistent. Write either "For each agent $i \in N$, each bundle $z_i \in Z_i$, and each price $p \in \Delta^{\ell-1}\ldots$," thereby helping us see that i is an agent, z_i a bundle, and p a price; or "For each $i \in N$, each $z_i \in Z_i$, and each $p \in \Delta^{\ell-1}\ldots$," if you feel we should know. But do not write "For each $i \in N$, each bundle $z_i \in Z_i$, and each $p \in \Delta^{\ell-1}\ldots$," because only one of the variables is preceded by a descriptive term.

In the more formal parts of the paper, such as the proofs, you can usually skip the extra words and use the second format.

5.5 Specify Precisely the Assumptions, or Particular Parts of Them, Used in Each Step

Do not write "The above assumptions imply that f is increasing" if you need only some of those assumptions to prove that f is increasing. It should be clear whether you mean all of the assumptions stated so far or only those discussed in the preceding paragraph. Write "Assumptions 3 and 4 imply that f is increasing." Even better, if you do not need Part (i) of Assumption 4, write "Assumption 3 and Part (ii) of Assumption 4 together imply that f is increasing."

It may not be enough to say that Theorem 3 follows from Lemmas 1 and 2. You may have to demonstrate how it does so.

Do not write "*A* and *B* imply *C* and *D*," if in fact "*A* implies *C* and *B* implies *D*." With a very small additional effort, you can be much more precise.

When you cite an earlier result, be as exact as possible. For classic theorems, refer to a textbook your readers are likely to be familiar with. This is especially important when a theorem exists in several forms; readers need to know which version you are using. You should also probably cite the English edition of a classic text instead of the translated version in another language, even if it is your own native language or one you know well. So write: "By the Brouwer fixed-point theorem (Debreu, 1959: 26)." Adding the page number is a nice touch suggested to me by Martha Stewart.

5.6   Don't Leave (Too Many) Steps to the Reader

Give your complete arguments. Some steps in a proof may involve standard manipulations and detract from your main point. Perhaps they should not be in the body of the paper but in an appendix. Just don't eliminate them. Readers may not be familiar with a derivation you have seen and performed hundreds of times. Having the option to assess the length of a step and recognize the names of familiar theorems on which it is based will help them check their own understanding of your logic, even without studying the details. In general, I do not like to see too much of the proof relegated to appendices. When I first look at a paper, I skip most of it anyway; if I decide to study it more seriously, I find it annoying to have to flip back and forth between the text and the appendix. While logical developments belong in the text proper, it is acceptable to file routine calculations, such as those involved in checking second-order conditions, in the appendix. Except for referees, almost no one checks these calculations, as there is rarely anything to learn from them. (Indeed, we hope that the referees did check them.)

5.7   Use a Consistent Writing Style

In the next few subsections I address several issues of style in the writing of proofs.

First, in a proof do not switch back and forth between first-person singular, third-person singular, first-person plural, and passive forms. If you summarize your paper as follows: "In section 3, I show that an equilibrium exists. In section 4, we establish uniqueness. To prove these

Figure 1.9
A Reader to Whom You Leave Too Many Steps Will Pick up Something Else To Read.
Do not leave steps to the reader. Will your weary reader really attempt to understand a proof where so many steps are left out?

results, it is assumed that preference relations are strictly convex. For the proof of the main theorem, one appeals to the Brouwer fixed-point theorem. Section 5 concludes," your readers will think you need psychiatric help. Are you *I* or *we*? Is it because these assumptions are embarrassing that you suddenly hide behind the passive form? Believe me, we all make embarrassing assumptions. And why do you let section 5 conclude when you did all the work? The passive form is found awkward by me, and our advice here is to have it replaced! *I* is perhaps too personal; between *I* and *we*, I usually choose *we*; but if you choose *I*, we will respect your choice.[30]

Similarly, do not travel back and forth between the present and future tenses. Don't write: "First, I prove existence. Then I will apply the

---

30. As a reader, I rather like the *I* form, which is more engaging, but I am not comfortable using it in formal papers. I use *I* here only because of the informal style I chose for this essay. Paradoxically, *we* is less obtrusive than *I*. *We* can also be interpreted as "I and the reader," whom you are taking along. But then be careful if you refer to "our previous work" that you mean you and your coauthor(s), not you and your reader.

theorem to exchange economies. I conclude with open questions." In most cases, using the present tense throughout, even when describing past literature, is just fine.[31]

In choosing the sex of your agents, it is difficult to be both consistent and fair. Certainly do not subject your consumers to sex change operations from paragraph to paragraph! In some situations, there are good solutions to the gender problem. For instance, two-person games are great for sexual equality. Make one player a male and the other a female. This will even facilitate talking about the game and help readers keep the players straight in their minds. It will also save you from the awkward *he or she, him or her, his or her*! These expressions are not elegant and I try to avoid them, but sometimes it is hard to come up with anything better. Alternatively, you may be able to refer to your agents in the plural (but remember my earlier advice that writing in the singular is often more precise). Or make one agent a firm or a household and refer to it as *it*.

Restructuring your sentence to avoid the pronoun problem is often possible: replace "If a consumer has quasi-linear preferences, the public-good component of his maximizing bundle is independent of his income" with "The public-good component of a consumer whose preferences are quasi-linear is independent of income."

The plural possessive with a singular subject is an abomination.

5.8 Be Consistent in Choosing Running Indices and Quantifications

Consistency in referring to running indices or quantifications is also important. If $N = \{1, \ldots, n\}$, do not write interchangeably "for all $i \in N$," or "for all $i \in \{1, \ldots, n\}$," or "for all $i = 1, \ldots, n$." Pick one formula and stick with it.

In most situations, the quantification for the set of agents is clear. If so, you may skip it and write "for all i." This helps reduce the density of symbols. In general, though, it is a good idea to indicate membership explicitly. Instead of "There exists z for which...," write "There exists $z \in Z$ for which ..." (Z being the set of feasible allocations, which you have previously defined). Therefore, when everything else is explicitly quantified, for style uniformity and aesthetic reasons, it bothers me a little not to see membership indicated for the set of agents—even if it is obvious that they come from N and not from Mars. So instead of "For all i such that...," I would write "For all $i \in N$ such that ..."

---

31. Grammarians call that the narrative (story-telling) present.

Incidentally, even though the notation $(O_1, \ldots, O_i, \ldots, O_n)$ seems to exclude the values 1 and n for the running index i, everyone will understand that they are included. If you write $(O_i)_{i \in N}$ you will lose the possible benefit—depending on your application—of having the list components spread out for all to see. Shortcuts of the form $(O_i)_{i \in N}$, $\sum_N x_i$, or $\prod_N x_i$, are indeed not always desirable. Writing $(O_1, \ldots, O_n)$, $x_1 + \cdots + x_n$, or $x_1 \times \cdots \times x_n$ sometimes helps.

Have one running index for each category of objects. For instance, do not use the same symbol for the running index for both commodities and agents. "Let $p_0 \equiv \min_i p_i$ and consider an arbitrary agent $i \in N$" is better rewritten as "Let $p_0 \equiv \min_\ell p_\ell$ and consider an arbitrary agent $i \in N$." In many situations, the choice of running indices will not matter, but in others it will. When describing the Lindahl mechanism, for example, you need to index prices by agents. So $p_0 \equiv \sum p_i$ is the price vector faced by the producers of the public goods when each consumer i faces the individual price vector p_i.

Finally, in a given expression do not use the same variable to refer to an object taken from some set and as an index running over the objects in the set: replace "For all $i \in N, x_i \le \sum_N a_i$" by "For all $i \in N, x_i \le \sum_N a_j$."

5.9 Don't Use Quantifiers in an English Sentence

Quantifiers should be reserved for mathematical expressions and should not appear in the middle of a text sentence. A sentence such as "Blah, blah, blah, $\forall x$ such that $P(x)$, blah, blah, blah $\exists y$ such that $Q(x, y)$ and blah, blah, blah" does not look good. Use English: "for all" and "there exists." If the mathematical statements introduced by the quantifiers are complex, pull the statements in mathematics out of the text and display them on separate lines, as follows: "Blah, blah ... blah, blah,

$$\forall x \text{ such that } P(x), \exists y \text{ such that } Q(x, y),$$

and blah, blah, blah."

Even though you do not want your text to be a mere translation of the mathematical statements in the proofs, the verbal parts of your paper should not leave the reader wondering about the quantifications needed to understand it. You can skip some of them to lighten your text, but make sure a reasonably prepared reader is bound to infer them from context. In formal statements, however (definitions, proofs), all quantifications should be explicit. (One of the side benefits of such explicitness is that taking the negation of a mathematical statement—an operation

Figure 1.10
Quantifiers as a Spice. Sprinkle your proofs with quantifiers. They will taste better.

you have to perform often—is a trivial task if the statement is properly
written, with no hidden quantifications.)

The only mathematical symbols that do not bother me in text are $\leq$,
$\subseteq$, and $\in$—and similar symbols like the strict inequalities, the strict in-
clusions, the preference statements, etc.—read as prepositions or verbs.
"Blah, blah, blah, since $x \geq y$, and $x \in A$, and therefore, blah, blah, blah,
f is continuous" is fine. But these symbols certainly should not appear
in the introduction or conclusion.

$\exists$ situations where it is convenient to quantify once and $\forall$[32]. For instance, open your proof by stating: "In what follows, S denotes an arbitrary element of Σ." Then the requirement that the function $F: \Sigma \to \mathbb{R}^2$
satisfies "for all $S \in \Sigma$, $F(S) > 0$" can simply be written as

POSITIVITY: $F(S) > 0$.[33]

32. See the problem with starting a sentence with a piece of mathematical notation (see
section 5.10)! When I wrote earlier that you should not put quantifiers in the middle of a
text sentence, I should have said "Do not put them anywhere in such a sentence."
33. Or "$F > 0$." By the way, do not place your footnote markers at the end of mathematical
expressions, as they will look like exponents. Placing them beyond the punctuation mark,
as the typographical convention requires, and as I have done here, helps. Nevertheless,

Journal editors will revise a sentence starting with a piece of mathematical notation. I agree with them that it does not look good, especially if the notation is lower case. "x designates an allocation" is not pretty. "I is the set of individuals" is not as bad because I is uppercase. (But what a grammatical provocation!).[34] Editors prefer "Let x designate an allocation."[35]

5.10   Show Clearly Where Each Proof Ends

Indicate where your proofs end. Use QED (*quod erat demonstrandum*) or Halmos's □ (for, I suppose, *quod erat quadrandum*).[36] Delete the redundant "This completes the proof," that precedes □ in your current draft.

5.11   If You Think a Step Is Obvious, Look Again

The following recommendations may seem to have as much to do with doing the proofs as with presenting them—but I don't see these as distinct activities.

Do not think that your own errors necessarily occur in the hard parts of your proofs (I should say, in what you think are the hard parts of your proofs). They may well have hidden in (what you think are) the easy parts, taking advantage of your overconfidence. After completing your

---

logic would sometimes dictate that the marker be attached to a word inside the clause or sentence that ends with a punctuation mark. Compare the marker for this footnote with the marker for note 32: the position of that marker did not create any ambiguity, as I am sure you did not think it was my intention to raise the universal quantifier to any power. Still, it did not look pretty.

The same problem arises with quotation marks. At the beginning of this note I wrote "$F > 0$." The rule is to write "$F > 0$." This is in agreement with logic if you think of the whole sentence, including the period that ends it, as being the unit that is being discussed. In other contexts, it may be the requirement "$F > 0$" that is under discussion but here—given that quotation marks look a little like the double prime symbol—I admit that placing them after the punctuation mark is preferable. Therefore, you should write something like: "the requirement "$F > 0$," stated in Section 2."

34. "I am the set of individuals" is a little pretentious though! Sounds like: "The set of individuals, c'est moi!"

35. Not that I agree with all of the conventions editors impose on us. In particular, their punctuation conventions do not all make sense. Being forced to end a sentence with "mechanism." is as painful to me as encountering expressions such as $\{(x + y\})$.

36. *Circulus*? What about a little circle to indicate the beginning of a proof, matching the little square that closes it?

paper, search for the words *clearly* and *obviously* and make sure that what you call clear and obvious is, if not clear and obvious, at least true.[37]

5.12   *Verify the Independence of Your Hypotheses*

For each hypothesis in each theorem, check whether you could proceed without it. Don't write "Under Assumptions A, B, and C, then D," if A and B together imply C, or if A and B together imply D.

Once after I put together a toy for one of my daughters I discovered some leftover parts in the box. Either these were replacement parts or I had done something wrong. (I will not tell you which but will say as a clue that there never are replacement parts in the box). Using the same logic, after you have written QED look in the box for stranded hypotheses. You might have made a mistake; but you might also be pleasantly surprised to find that you can actually prove your theorem without differentiability. Wouldn't you be thrilled to discover that your result applied to Banach lattices (which you didn't even know existed two weeks ago) whereas you thought you were working in boring old n-dimensional Euclidean space?

Occasionally, you will be unable to show that a certain hypothesis is necessary for the proof and unable to conclude without it either. This is an uncomfortable situation that should keep you up late at night.

A given hypothesis may be the conjunction of several more elementary ones. In that case, try to work without each of the components in turn. If you have shown that "Under compactness of the set X, conclusion C holds," don't simply check that without compactness C might not hold anymore. Instead, ask whether "Under boundedness of X, C holds" and whether "Under closedness of X, C holds."

5.13   *Explore All Possible Variants of Your Results*

If you have proved Statement P, "A and B together imply C," do not stop there. Find out whether similar statements hold when you replace A with the closely related conditions A', A^0, and $\tilde{A}$, or replace B with B' and B^*, or C with C^0. Knowing P is not enough. Discover as many statements as possible that are close to P and are also true, as well as statements that are close to P but are not true. Indicate as a remark the main variants of P and keep to yourself the least-significant ones.

---

37. Don't deduce from this suggestion, however, that simply deleting every *clearly* and *obviously* will eliminate all your errors.

It is just as useful to understand the various statements similar to the one you are proving that could be true but are not as to understand the statement you are proving. It may even be more useful.

By the way, if you conjectured that a certain statement is true but are having trouble proving it, try proving its negation. Either you will be successful and save yourself the embarrassment of proving something that is not true or, if your initial intuition was indeed correct, you will almost certainly gain useful insights into the proof of your conjecture that you may not have obtained otherwise.

6   Use Pictures

Even simple pictures can be of considerable help in making your paper easily understandable and you seminar presentation more vivid. Of course, a picture is not a substitute for a proof, and the proof should be (in general) understandable without one. But an illustration may convey the main idea of the proof and, thereby, cut down by half (probably much more) the time needed for readers to understand it. Again, remember the hundreds of little diagrams you drew on the way to your results. Also, think about why, when you meet the author of a paper that interested you and ask for an explanation of some point that confused you, the author almost always says: "The argument is actually very simple. Let me draw a little picture to show you how it works."

In addition to illustrating definitions and steps of proofs, figures also provide relief from long verbal or algebraic developments. Altogether, they make a paper more inviting.

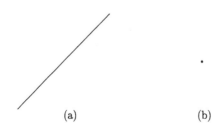

(a)   (b)

Figure 1.11
Even Simple Pictures Can Be a Great Help in Understanding Proofs. (a) Picture of a line. (b) Picture of a point.

6.1   Prepare the Ground

I only recently learned to create figures in LaTeX, and I was astounded to discover how much one could do with just five or six commands. I strongly suggest that you try. Here are a few lessons I drew from my still-limited experience.

Prepare the ground. Draw a sketch of your figure on paper to see what configuration of the elements looks best. This first step may require that you do some calculations—perhaps to identify the exact coordinates of where two important lines intersect. Although this preparation is necessary, don't calculate everything ahead of time. Only printing out a picture will show whether you have left enough room between two curves to insert some needed notation, whether a nonconvexity is sufficiently well marked to be noticed, or whether labels are unambiguous and not too tight. Construct your picture in stages. Begin with its critical components and print it. Make the required modifications and print it again. Add the secondary curves or points. Print it again. You may then have to make more changes to the first elements: three points should not be lined up, a curve should not be concave, two lines should not be parallel or perpendicular, and so on, without reasons.

Draw the figures approximately the size you want them to appear in published form. Reducing a figure that is too large, or enlarging one that is too small, will not always affect the lettering in similar fashion: the lettering may end up being too crowded, or too loose, or too small.

Add comments to the file indicating what each line of code refers to. It is very hard to find one's way around a picture file to make corrections.

If you have a series of figures indicating the stages of a constructive proof—for instance, one presenting the basic data of an economy, and two others illustrating Steps 1 and 2—proceed backward and do the most complicated one first. If you start with the simplest one, you will have no problem specifying the data it represents and making it easy to decipher; but when you need to add to it to illustrate Step 1, and then Step 2, you will find that some of this data has to be changed. For example, you may not have enough room to label an item that only appears later, whereas if you had drawn some of the initial elements differently you would have had plenty of space. Redrawing two indifference curves to increase the spacing between them will force you to redo the first picture, and the time you spent perfecting it will have been wasted. So do the last figure first. Then, remove from the file the lines of code for the curves, points, and labels that pertain to the later stages of proof, leaving only the basic data of your economy: that is your first figure.

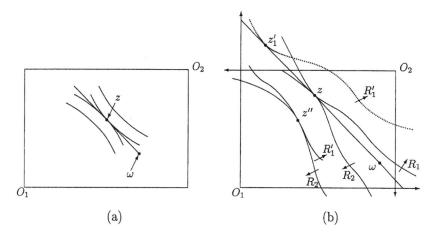

Figure 1.12
The Wrong and Right Ways to Draw an Edgeworth Box. (a) Do you call that an Edgeworth box? (b) *That's* an Edgeworth box.

6.2 The Edgeworth Box

The Edgeworth box depicts a two-good, two-agent exchange economy. We use it in our classrooms to introduce most of the concepts of equilibrium theory, welfare economics, implementation, and so on and to convey the main ideas of proofs. It is such a useful expository device that a few additional pointers on its use are justified.

One common mistake is to draw the box as a simple rectangle (figure 1.12a), which has the unfortunate consequence of obscuring boundary issues. The feasible set is, of course, adequately represented as a rectangle. However, certain properties of allocation rules involve information about preference relations outside the feasible set, and a number of rules depend on such information—even though they take values only within the feasible set. (Our central rule, the *Walrasian correspondence*, is an example.[38])

Starting from two copies of the two-dimensional commodity space, each containing the relevant information about the preference relation and the endowment of agent 1 or agent 2, you construct the Edgeworth box by rotating agent 2's consumption space 180 degrees and sliding it until the two endowment points coincide. This operation defines a rectangle of the correct size. Note that the two pairs of axes extend

---

38. I use this term to designate the rule that associates with each economy the allocations obtained at a competitive equilibrium.

beyond the rectangle; so do many of the indifference curves and—if your purpose is to explain the notion of a Walrasian equilibrium—the budget sets. In fact, if prices are not equilibrium prices, an agent may well maximize his preference relation in his budget sets at points where his consumption of some good exceeds the social endowment of it. This point does not belong to the Edgeworth box (agent 1 in figure 1.12b maximizes the preference relation R_1' at z_1'). Remember that an important feature of the Walrasian correspondence is that agents need not know the aggregate feasibility constraints when performing these individual maximizations. To talk about implementation you also have to be careful about boundaries; drawing indifference curves that extend beyond the rectangle will help you keep them in mind.

Label figures as completely as possible. Label the allocations, the supporting prices, and the endowments. In similar figures (for example, a series illustrating the steps of a proof), position similar labels in similar places. To indicate the efficiency of an allocation, it often helps to shade the upper contour sets in the neighborhood of that allocation. Label a few indifference curves for each agent (some redundancy is useful). If you assume convexity of preference relations, and if in fact you

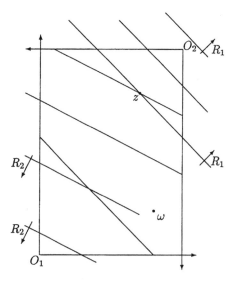

Figure 1.13
An Edgeworth Box for Linear Preference Relations. Draw indifference curves that extend beyond the feasible set. (Is this the first Edgeworth box in the history of economic analysis that is taller than it is wide?)

draw strictly convex indifference curves, who owns which indifference curve will be unambiguous. But if you do not make that assumption—you may very well work with linear preference relations or nonconvex ones—ownership will not always be so clear. In Figure 1.13, in which indifference curves are linear, I attempted to show that agent 1 is the one with the relatively greater affinity for good 1 (that is, the one whose indifference curves are steeper). I did so by

1. Drawing one of this agent's indifference curves in a region that could not be part of agent 2's consumption space (this is the small segment to the northeast of O_2), since for agent 2 that region corresponds to negative consumptions of some of the goods;
2. Labeling agent 1's indifference curves with the notation R_1;
3. Indicating the direction of increasing satisfaction with arrows.

Avoid unnecessary arrows such as the ones pointing to ω and z in Figure 1.12a. You can almost always position labels close to the items they designate without creating ambiguities; use an arrow only when there is not enough room to put the label close to the object, which typically occurs when labels are too long.[39]

Recently, I became curious about whether Edgeworth himself would pass my Edgeworth box test and looked up his *Mathematical Psychics*. His Figure 1.14a (1881:28) is the closest thing to an Edgeworth box I found in the book. According to all the secondary sources I consulted, nothing in his other works looks even remotely like an Edgeworth box.[40]

The case of Bowley is similar. There is one box in his 1924 classic, *Mathematical Groundwork of Economics* (figure 1.14b), but it does not meet my standards. It should not meet yours, either.

Pareto's box (figure 1.14c) has the familiar appearance of the box that appears in all modern textbooks, but he did very little with the device.

---

39. Look at the map of your city and you will see that all the streets—there are hundreds of them—are labeled without arrows and yet are unambiguously identifiable. If the mapmaker could do it, you surely can do without arrows in your Edgeworth box.

40. Tarascio (1972) and Jaffé (1974) looked this up before me. Jaffé writes: "It may come as a surprise, to those who rely exclusively on secondary sources of information on past analytic achievements, to learn that nowhere in Edgeworth's published writing is there anything resembling what is so frequently referred to as an 'Edgeworth box diagram.' To my knowledge, the earliest adumbration of a true box diagram is found on page 288 (Figure 16) of the fifth instalment of Vilfredo Pareto's article, 'Considerazioni sui principii fondamentali dell'economia pura,' which appeared in October 1893, twelve years after the publication of Edgeworth's *Mathematical Psychics*."

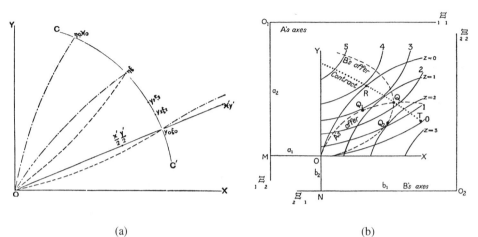

(a)   (b)

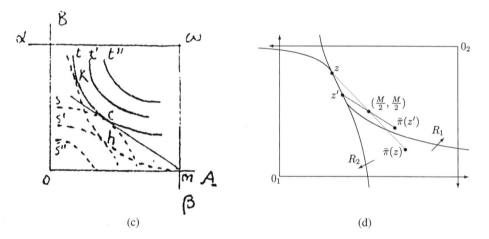

(c)   (d)

Figure 1.14
On the Evolution of the Edgeworth Box. In the top two diagrams, the contract curve is downward sloping. (a) Edgeworth's box; (b) Bowley's box (note choice of origins); (c) Pareto's box; (d) a late-twentieth-century model.

7 Conclusion

If you follow all the above recommendations, you will be pleased with yourself, your seminar audiences will be enlightened, your classmates will be impressed, your parents will be proud, and you will land a job in a top-five department. But most importantly—and here, I speak as an adviser—your adviser will be happy with you.

I readily admit that each of the points I make does not amount to much, and you could ask "What's the big deal if I ignore it?" You are right about any one of them individually. Small imperfections, however, when added together, will take your paper over the line that separates those that can be understood from those that cannot. An Archimedean principle is at work here. If you ignore all these suggestions, you will lose your readers or your seminar audiences much earlier than necessary. In fact, you too will be confused.

Be realistic. Very few readers can take the time to understand everything in your paper, and a large fraction of your seminar audience will have only a vague idea of what you are talking about when you are halfway through your presentation. Every bit you do to improve your text or seminar paper will keep the attention of a few people a little longer.

If you are used to certain notational conventions, or terminology, or ways of structuring a proof, they almost certainly seem to you the best—and perhaps the only ones worth considering. Yet, you should be open-minded enough to experiment with other formulations. Only after giving them a genuine test can you decide which one is truly best. The first few times you use a new piece of notation or a new term or a new format, it will appear strange to you. Give it a chance. That means actually doing the work, not just thinking about doing it. Only by writing out, printing, and looking at the different versions of a definition you are considering will you be able to judge which is the most transparent.

Let some time elapse between revisions. If your paper is so familiar to you that you essentially know it by heart, you will never discover your mistakes. Let it sit in a drawer for a while; when you pick it up again, you will see immediately how it can be improved. You certainly should not send to a journal on Monday a paper you spent the whole weekend revising. On Tuesday you will discover several imperfections. On Wednesday, you will spot additional problems and begin to wish you had looked it over once more before mailing it. On Thursday, you will come across an error in a proof and send an e-mail asking the editor to please wait for a revised version. Not the best way to gain an editor's trust. If, on the other hand, your last two rounds of revisions were separated by a week and you found only two typos in the latest one, go ahead. Correct the typos and submit the paper.

If you are invited to revise it, take the various recommendations of the associate editor and referees very seriously. You probably have already made other changes in response to comments you received after sending the paper to the journal. Keep a copy of the version you submitted so that you can find the specific pages, paragraphs or lines mentioned by the referees in their comments. Along with your revision, send a letter indicating how you have answered each of the referees' comments. If the referees made contradictory suggestions, in your reply to them make them aware of their divergent opinions and explain how you handled the discrepancy.

It is never too late to make corrections; you can make them even after your paper has been accepted. Then, you should bring the editor's attention to the fact. However, such postacceptance corrections should not be substantial. If necessary, you can make them on the galley proofs, where you will almost certainly have to update some references. It's best, of course, not to find yourself in that situation; but if you do discover an important error, prevent it from getting into print. You may even have to withdraw your paper.

After many revisions, your paper has become like a smooth and shiny pebble that fits snugly into the palm of your hand. It has been accepted by a top journal, and you just sent in the final version. At this point, treat yourself to a box of Belgian chocolates. And if you have found my recommendations useful, please save one for me.

8   Related Literature

When I circulated this essay, several readers gave me references to similar pedagogical advice written by mathematicians. I am happy to report that these authors's recommendations are not always contrary to mine. Paul Halmos's essay in Steenrod et al. (1981) is the most often cited, and deservedly so. I also found Nicholas Higham (1993) particularly helpful. Leslie Lamport's LaTeX manual (1986) is beautiful. (I am even considering forgiving the author for the maxim "All axioms are dull.")

The Elements of Style by William Strunk and E. B. White (1959) is the best-known general writer's guide, and I also strongly recommend William Zinsser's *Writing to Learn* (1988). The *Merriam-Webster Dictionary of English Usage* (1994) is an invaluable source on the subject. Deirdre McCloskey (2000) addresses a number of important stylistic issues that come up in the writing of economics. Eugene Rasmussen (1999) offers useful advice on presenting empirical research.

The dictionary I recommend is *The American Heritage Dictionary of the English Language* (1992). Although it is one of the few not to invoke

Webster's name, it is vastly superior to any of its comparably priced competitors found in college bookstores. It offers delightful notes on synonyms, regional differences, word histories, and word usage. For spelling conventions, editors often use *Merriam-Webster's Collegiate Dictionary* (latest edition).

A text to use as a model is Gérard Debreu's monograph, *The Theory of Value* (1959).

9   References

The way I chose to present these references is my small contribution to the fight against alphabetism (discrimination on the basis of one's position in the alphabet).[41]

Zinsser, William. *Writing to Learn*. New York: Harper & Row, 1988.

Van Zandt, Timothy. *PSTricks: PostScript Macros for Generic T$_E$X*. Users' Guide. 1997. (http://zandtwerk.insead.fr/tex/html)

Tarascio, Vincent J. "A Correction: On the Genealogy of the So-called Edgeworth-Bowley Diagram." *Western Economic Journal* 10 (1972): 193–97.

Strunk Jr., William, and E. B. White. *The Elements of Style*. New York: Macmillan, 1959.

Rasmussen, Eugene, "Aphorisms on Writing, Speaking, and Listening." Bloomington: Indiana University, 1999 (mimeographed).

Pareto, Vilfredo. "Considerazioni sui principii fondamentali dell'economia pura." October 1893. (Cited in Jaffé 1974.)

Merriam-Webster's Dictionary of English Usage. Springfield, Mass.: Merriam-Webster, 1994.

Merriam-Webster's Collegiate Dictionary, 10th ed. Springfield, Mass.: Merriam-Webster, 1993.

Manguel, Antony. "Point of Order." *New York Times,* April 18, 1999.

McCloskey, Deirdre N. *Economical Writing*. Prospect Heights, Ill.: Waveland Press, 2000.

Lamport, Leslie. *LAT$_E$X*. Reading, Mass.: Addison-Wesley, 1986.

Jaffé, William. "Edgeworth's Contract Curve. Part 1: A Propaedeutic Essay in Clarification," *History of Political Economy* 6 (1974): 343–59.

Higham, Nicholas J. *Handbook for the Mathematical Sciences*. Philadelphia: Society for Industrial and Applied Mathematics, 1993.

Halmos, Paul R. "How to Write Mathematics." In *How to Write Mathematics,* Norman E. Steenrod, Paul E. Halmos, Marcellus M. Schiffer, and Jean-Alexandre Dieudonné, eds. Providence: American Mathematical Society, 1981.

---

41. To be consistent, I should say "omegapsism," or rather, since after all I am using Latin letters, "zyism."

Grafton, Anthony. *The Footnote.*[42] Cambridge: Harvard University Press, 1997.[43]

Goossens, Michael, Sebastian Rahtz, and Frank Mittelbach. *LATEX Graphics Companion: Illustrating Documents with TEX and PostScript.* Reading, Mass.: Addison-Wesley, 1997.

Edgeworth, Francis Y. *Mathematical Psychics: An Essay on the Application of Mathematics to the Moral Sciences.* London: C. K. Paul, 1881.

Debreu, Gerard. *The Theory of Value.* New Haven: Yale University monograph, 1959.

Bowley, Arthur L. *The Mathematicial Groundwork of Economics: An Introductory Treatise.* Oxford: Clarendon Press, 1924.

American Heritage Dictionary, 3d ed. Boston: Houghton Mifflin, 1992.

A Quiz

The first person who identifies the origins of the following citations gets a prize.

1. *"Erreur, tu n'es pas un mal."* (subsection 1.3)
2. "Therefore, I can clearly not choose the wine in front of me." (subsection 5.1)
3. "Hernandez and Fernandez." (subsection 4.13)
4. "Qfwfq and Xlthlx." (subsection 4.7)

---

42. A Curious History
43. Footnote 42 is part of the title, just as I reproduced it, without punctuation (and of course, it is not footnote 42 in Grafton's book).

2   Giving Talks

If you are giving your first talk and feel nervous, this essay may help a little. Although in the preceding chapter I touched on a few questions relevant to oral presentations, I focused it primarily on written exposition. In this chapter, I address issues specific to oral communication.

The exact form of your talk will depend on whether it is a job talk, a seminar paper given at a university where you already have a job, or a conference presentation. In a job talk your priority is showing what you have accomplished. Once you have landed a job, you will not only want to advertise your work but also learn from experts. Irrespective of the circumstances, keep in mind that you will have, essentially, a captive audience and that the time spent preparing to make the best possible impression is always well spent.

1   How Is an Oral Presentation Different from a Paper? How Is It the Same?

Most rules of good writing apply to oral presentations as well. Whether sitting at your desk or standing in front of a blackboard, clarity should be your objective. And simplicity is always the best means of achieving it. What you should write to make your text easy to read is also what you should say to make your seminar easy to follow, although you may express it slightly differently (as spoken English is not quite the same as written English).

Begin by telling listeners what issues you are addressing. Place your work in the context of the existing literature; point to what we have learned from this earlier work, and how its insufficiencies motivated you in your investigation. State the long-term objectives of your research program, the general goals of your paper, the specific questions it addresses, and why these questions are interesting and important. You do not, however, have to outline the structure of your presentation in great detail, and you certainly do not need to announce your results at the outset. Simply indicate briefly the direction you are heading. Choose plain language and transparent notation.

However, written and oral communications differ in a number of important ways. Each has certain advantages and limitations, as the next subsections explain. Learn to exploit the benefits and avoid the dangers of each.

1.1 Advantages of Oral Presentations

Many of the following advantages of oral presentations stem from the fact that during your talk you are in a sense a teacher and so may use the sort of didactic devices you use in a classroom.

- Oral presentations are live. Communication is most effective when face to face.

- Unfolding over time, they have a dynamic structure that a text lacks. They are a better means to show how an argument develops.

- In a presentation, you have a wide variety of media at your disposal—blackboards, transparencies, handouts—and can encourage listeners' attention by going back and forth between them. (Just don't overdo it). And, of course, you possess that unique instrument of communication, your voice.

- You also have choices in formatting, structuring, summarizing, showing logical relations, and suggesting connections that are not available or are less effectively implemented in print. Use colors to attract attention to something important, or simply to provide visual stimulation. Draw sketches to indicate the geometric properties of the objects you are studying, and use diagrams to show the steps of a proof. Present your assumptions, conclusions, and the directions for future research in the form of lists. A very useful method of revealing structure, lists are used only occasionally in a journal article, whereas most of your transparencies can be composed of lists. Icons and menus have made computers accessible to the general public much more effectively than instructions written in complete sentences would ever have done. In a presentation, you will most successfully communicate your ideas and results in the same way: through pictures and lists.[1]

- You can be informal in your tone and style of delivery. In fact, not only can you be informal, you have to abandon the formalism of your printed text. You can tell a joke or an anecdote that would not work in print. You can express emotions: surprise that equilibrium exists, disappointment that it is not efficient, or excitement that it is. You should certainly show enthusiasm about your work. A talk is not the place to let yourself be overcome by whatever doubts you may have about its importance. If you appear unconvinced, you will probably not engage your audience. I do not suggest that you should be cocky— in fact, I advise against it. But other things being equal, pretending excitement a little is not a bad idea. Do not begin with an apology for not really settling the issue you intended to resolve.

- The chance to interact with the audience is another major advantage of the oral presentation. The prospect may frighten you now, but with time you will find that such exchanges can be fun and productive. However, there are lines not to cross. Do not, for example, put listeners on the spot by asking which strategy they would choose in a game you have just displayed—especially if your next transparency shows why the most common choice is wrong. Also it is something of a tradition in economics seminars to use specific members of the audience as generic agents, but the device is often awkward or tiresome. If you say "Suppose Dick has low ability and Jane has high ability" (Dick and Jane are sitting in the front row), Jane may be initially pleased with the attention—after all, you gave her high ability but Dick will probably have mixed feelings. If you refer to them in these terms too often, they will soon both wish you had picked someone else; and they will certainly be uncomfortable if, on one of those occasions when you mention their names, you startle them in the middle of a little snooze.

- You choose the pace of your presentation and control what your audience knows at every point. In a printed paper, by contrast, individual readers will work their way around it in their own particular fashion, over which you have no control.

---

1. The list format is typical of how-to manuals. Although not elegant literature, it is particularly suited to giving recommendations. That's why I make much use of it in this essay.

- Oral presentations are more conducive than papers to discussing the paths not taken, the reasons why, and the lessons you drew from failures. The possibility of talking a little about the personal history of your work, recounting how your thinking evolved over time and how your results gained in generality, is one of the benefits of a talk over a paper. Show how you got interested in your problem and relate the elementary observations that led you to your first conjectures. Explain what you learned from various obstacles encountered, how you obtained your initial results, and how they gave you the crucial insights that put you on the glorious road to your general theorems and their proofs. However, though much can often be learned from false starts and misconceptions, resist the temptation to go down too many dead ends, no matter how fascinating they are to you. Limit yourself to those that are instructive.

- The standards of mathematical rigor in an oral presentation are somewhat more relaxed than those applied to a journal article, which is another advantage. You can sketch a proof or present a simplified version of it that only holds in special cases.

- For many of the reasons just enumerated, talks are particularly well suited to present work in progress.

1.2   Difficulties of Oral Presentations

The advantages or oral presentations described above are partially offset by a number of disadvantages, several of which are simply their flip sides.

- If English is not your native language, oral presentations may strain your abilities. Your accent will get in the way, especially if you are tired or nervous. You may find it difficult to pronounce critical words you have no problem spelling. Even if your written English is good, you are not likely to be as fluent a speaker as your Anglophone classmates. And you will not achieve a smooth delivery comparable to your polished written work. In an article, you can compensate for your imperfect English by devoting an essentially unbounded amount of time to revisions, but no such substitution is available in a conference or seminar presentation. You may have as little as twenty minutes to present your argument—and never more than an hour and a half.

- Moreover, you cannot possibly present as much information in a seminar as you can in a paper, and it is no use trying. Most of the fine points will have to go, and perhaps entire sections of your paper. A conference format will force you to be even more selective; you will have to limit yourself to a small part of your paper. Just make sure the audience gets your main message.

- People understand at different rates, and readers proceed at their own individual pace. When speaking you will have to choose a speed to accommodate everyone. Inevitably, you will be too slow for some and too fast for others.

- Time is experienced very differently by a speaker and the audience. You may think your presentation is going very quickly, but it is likely that when you are only halfway through it, many people will have already looked discreetly at the clock. It is much easier to speak for an hour and a half than to listen for that long. The speaker seems to be doing the work, but it is really the listeners who do so.

- Facing an audience requires you to be psychologically prepared and calls on completely different resources than those you relied on to write your paper. But be reassured that even if you are not one of the lucky few who feels immediately at ease in this kind of situation, your confidence will grow from presentation to presentation and eventually you will overcome your stage fright. This trivial observation won't help you at your workshop next week, but here is one that might: my own postpresentation conversations with speakers suggest that in general they felt more nervous than they appeared to the audience.

2 Preparing Yourself

My next recommendation is apparently paradoxical: Never put yourself in the position of having to explain something you have never explained before. One reason is obvious: the more often you do something, the better you will do it the next time. The second reason is perhaps less obvious, but it is even more important: you cannot possibly understand something until you have explained it to someone else. (I exaggerate here, but only a little.)

You are responsible for every aspect of your paper, and you should be able to explain it in a variety of ways—either informally, or with all the details of the proofs, and anywhere in between. Do not believe the person who claims to have understood something if he or she cannot explain it to you. If you truly understand an argument, you can explain it. To a stranger to the field, you can at least explain the main idea. Not having enough time is no excuse; that only affects the amount of detail you can provide. Be ready to describe your research in the five minutes of a hallway conversation, in the standard twenty minutes of a formal interview, in an hour over lunch, or in the hour and a half of a seminar. No matter how long you have, there has to be an optimal way of using that time. If you had only a few seconds, what would be the key words? If allowed one sentence to summarize your contribution, what would it be? In five minutes, what would you say? What is the central theorem? What is its most critical assumption? How would your answers to someone familiar with your specialty differ from your answers to someone in another field?

2.1   The Benefits of Explaining Aloud

If you should not trust that your proof is correct until you have written it down, you should also not trust that what you wrote down is correct until you have tested it in front of a live audience. In particular, do not think that a step is really trivial if you have not worked through it aloud at least once and heard your audience confirm that it is trivial. I am sure you have had the experience, when starting to describe a result to someone, of being stuck right away at a point you thought was completely obvious. The converse has also happened to you: having stalled in your research, you called on a friend for help, and immediately found the solution to the problem as you began explaining it. Describing your research to another person often brings out some previously unnoticed difficulty or that elusive piece that solves a puzzle. It works even when your listener knows little about your field and, even, remains silent. You feel like a fool for bothering your friend. Don't worry. Just keep doing it (and return the favor). It happens to everybody. Ideally, of course, it shouldn't happen in a seminar, which is why you need to practice with your friends first.

2.2   The Benefits of Practice

Before your first job-market seminar, you will have a number of opportunities to speak in progressively more and more public forums; first facing your classmates and adviser; then in your departmental seminar series; and perhaps at one or two conferences. Take advantage of these occasions and learn from them. Be attuned to the reactions of your audiences. You will discover that certain aspects of your work you expected to explain easily are not so easy after all—or at least not for everyone. Conversely, certain developments you thought difficult to explain went over surprisingly well. Use the seminar opportunities you have to experiment with alternative presentation strategies and never be satisfied with what you did on the last occasion; no matter how many times you have given a paper, you will discover something to make your presentation better.

By repeatedly explaining something, you are creating a mental "file" of sentences ready for easy retrieval. Eventually you will approach the optimal way of sequencing the components of a definition, identify which of its variables you need to name to make it easily understood, and so on. From then on, you will not have to think about these issues when you introduce the definition, leaving your mind free to compose your next sentence.

When practicing, time yourself. Estimate how long each of your possible points will take to discuss so that you can decide what to present and what to skip. Incidentally, underestimating how long an explanation will take is by far the most common error presenters make. Ask your host before you fly out (not when halfway through your talk) how long their seminars are. (An hour and a half is almost universal, but make sure.) Check periodically to see whether you are on track. Place your watch on the desk in front of you and check it discreetly (an analog watch will allow you to be more discreet). I have often stayed in a seminar room after the talk formally ended to question a speaker who got me particularly interested in a subject, but most of us consider it a cardinal sin not to finish on time, and all the readers of earlier versions of this essay suggested that I emphasize that point. On the other hand, no one will hold it against you if you finish early.

A presentation has logistical aspects to which you must also pay attention. Inspect the room where you will speak. Check whether the blackboard is large enough for some long formulae you want to exhibit (blackboards vary widely in size). Is chalk or colored chalk handy? Are markers for whiteboard available, and are they not out of ink? Don't count on your host to necessarily think about these details, nor to provide you with new markers if the ones you start with are inadequate—leaving you no choice but to proceed with ink that is nearly invisible. If you check them before you begin speaking, you will have a better chance that something can be done about the situation. Also, test the projector and learn to operate it. If there are several blackboards, you may be able to come to the room ahead of time to write down a long formula or a few steps of an algorithm or draw a complicated graph. But do that only if you can cover up what you write until you need it; otherwise it will be distracting. Besides, your goal should not be to do more, but to do better. If certain figures would be difficult for you to reproduce well on the blackboard, put them on transparencies.

3   Facing the Audience

In preparing your talk, think about what members of your audience are likely to know about your field, how to interest them in a topic that in most cases bears no relation to what they are working on, and how to sustain that interest throughout your talk. If you can offer them something useful to their own work—say a technique or a concept not limited to your particular application—emphasize that aspect of your work.

A talk is not a paper. The organization of your presentation, in particular, need not be that of your paper. Readers can go back and forth between different sections of your paper; and although listeners can certainly ask you to return to an earlier point, they can do so only a few times. Organize your presentation so that they won't have to.

3.1   What Can You Expect the Audience to Know?

Most listeners will not have read your paper in any detail before your talk, even if it was distributed ahead of time—as it would be in a job-interview talk. (At a conference, it will be up to you to bring copies.) Although many people may have skimmed it quickly, they probably won't be familiar with it or your other work. Present all essential features of your model and all essential definitions, even those you can legitimately assume they have seen before. Similarly, do not assume they are familiar with your notation, even if it is standard in the field.

3.2   Looking Backward and Forward

Briefly place your work in the context of your entire research *program*. Think of the opening shots of a movie: the camera starts high above the city, descends to a neighborhood, approaches a building, and miraculously moves through a wall and into the room where two characters are having a conversation—thus setting the stage for the drama that will unfold. This successive narrowing of frames is how you should introduce your paper and explain how it fits into the existing literature. At the end of your presentation, smoothly pull the camera back away again and conclude with some comments of a general nature.

Short introductions are preferable. How short surely depends on the paper itself, but a few minutes generally suffice. Do not attempt to provide details about your model at the outset, because you will not be able to explain it completely enough to help the audience understand exactly what you are doing. Listeners won't know whether to wait for a later clarification or ask a question now. The best way to preempt the unnecessary questions about your model that an informal description of it may generate—unnecessary because you will eventually give all the details—is to simply close the introduction and give them right away. Also, keep the literature survey short.

Telling the audience where you are headed does not mean announcing your results in the beginning. A little suspense will help keep people interested.

Do not promise too much. Listeners will either be disappointed or will not believe you and will keep challenging you as you go along.

Having been engaged for several months by a specific problem and buried in its technical details, you are in danger of losing perspective and forgetting how marginal it is to other people's interests. No one in the audience may have read any of the three or four papers that are the foundation on which you built. An understanding of them may be necessary to appreciate your own contribution; in such cases, your explanation must include their crucial results. Almost certainly, you were forced to work under assumptions that limited the scope of your paper; for people who already think of your area as but a small corner of the vast subject we call economics, your results are bound to appear of narrow interest.

You need, therefore, to think about how to convince such individuals that your findings are significant. Help them see the difficulties involved in reaching more general conclusions. Demonstrating the complications you encountered will help listeners accept that you could not be expected to have solved your problem with much greater generality. And don't be overly apologetic for the inevitable limitations of your paper. Of course, you should not be happy with your restrictive assumptions; and, yes, you should do your best to relax them. But you are not the first author who has had to settle for a limited answer rather than the desired broader one. As my colleague Lionel McKenzie once exclaimed in defense of a speaker, "Other people's assumptions are always too strong." If some one criticizes you for not taking into account incentive effects, or ignoring uncertainty, and so on, be reassured: at some time or other we have made the absurd assumption that all agents live infinitely many periods, or all have Cobb-Douglas preferences, or have no problem homing in on that particular Nash equilibrium.

The assumptions under which one commonly operates vary from field to field; what is important is that you know why the ones in your field are particularly critical to your area, though perhaps not to others. The mere fact that a limiting assumption is standard in your field is not a defense for imposing it. It is standard for one or several reasons: it allows for a closed-form solution to some system of equations; or it rules out income effects or strategic complications; and so on. These are the reasons why you, too, made the assumption, and you should be ready to explain them. The fact that your adviser suggested an assumption is not an adequate reason either. You need to know why your adviser did so.

3.3   Forgetting

A benefit of transparencies is that they remind you of everything you wanted to say. But forgetting is not necessarily all bad, provided that at some point you remember what you left out. It may even be useful, although a little risky, if what you omitted is important. It gives you a chance to emphasize the point: "Oh, of course! I forgot to tell you that existence of equilibrium holds *only* under the critical assumption of convexity of preferences. Otherwise, counterexamples can easily be found, and here is one." (The reason it is risky to forget is that you may forget for good.)

Pretending to forget something is also an effective way to bring attention to it. The danger is that someone in the audience may notice that it is missing before you have a chance to "remember" it, turning your scam into an embarrassment. To protect yourself from such a possibility, you can announce, "In stating my next theorem, I will leave a crucial hypothesis blank for a moment." If you do not feel comfortable with this sort of stratagem, don't try it right away. Eventually you will acquire the confidence to use it. The same comment applies to the next suggestions. Think about using them in future presentations to help you refine your skills as a speaker.

THEOREM 1

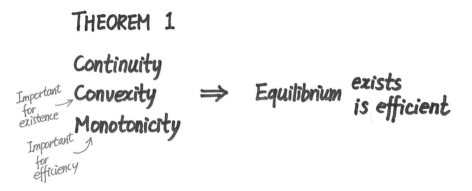

Continuity

Important for existence → Convexity $\Rightarrow$ Equilibrium exists is efficient

Monotonicity

Important for efficiency ↗

Plate 1

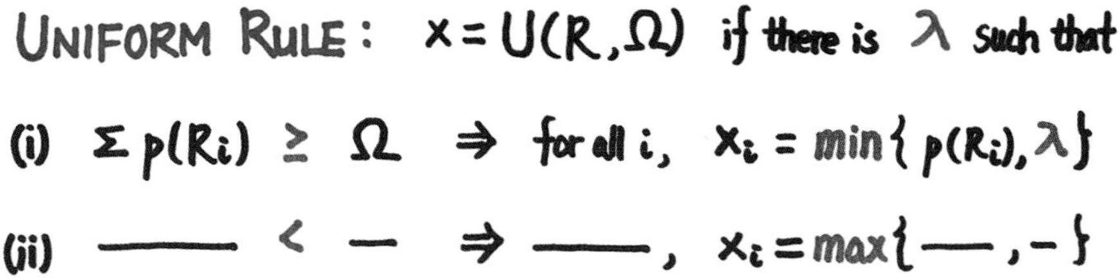

UNIFORM RULE: $x = U(R, \Omega)$ if there is λ such that

(i) $\sum p(R_i) \geq \Omega \Rightarrow$ for all i, $x_i = \min\{p(R_i), \lambda\}$

(ii) $\underline{\quad\quad} < - \Rightarrow \underline{\quad\quad}$, $x_i = \max\{\underline{\quad}, -\}$

Plate 2

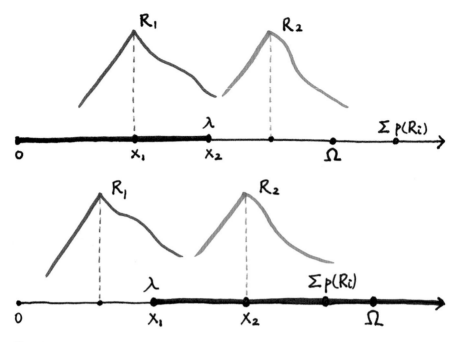

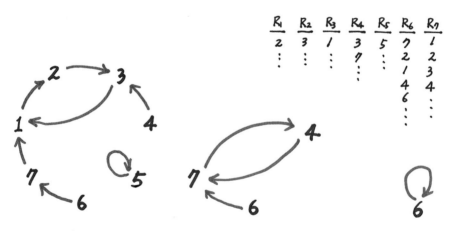

Plate 3

Plate 4

3.4 Making Mistakes

Deliberately making mistakes, then pointing out how easily one can be misled is another good way of bringing attention to something important. Of course, you will also make unintended errors, and you need to learn how to deal with them. Whether you or someone in the audience realizes your mistake first, acknowledge it and correct it as well as you can. Everyone makes mistakes, and everyone makes elementary mistakes. A mistake may be instructive, in which case turn it into an opportunity to gain new knowledge and earn the admiration of the audience for the style and grace with which you landed on your feet.

3.5 Digressing

Nothing is wrong with digressing from your main point once in a while—that is one more way in which a talk differs from a paper. In fact, I recommend doing so occasionally. Brief changes of pace will help listeners sit still for an hour and a half. Do not, however, lose sight of your goal, which is to present your work (See figure 2.1). Instructive digressions, such as a story that seems peripheral to your main point

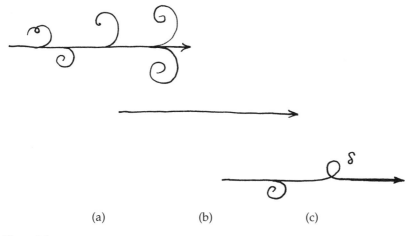

(a)   (b)   (c)

Figure 2.1
Good Digressions and Bad Digressions. (a) If you digress too often, listeners will get distracted and miss your main message. Besides, you may waste too much time and have to rush to deliver it. (b) Never digressing makes for a dry, and perhaps boring, presentation. (c) Occasional digressions, by varying the pace of your presentation, make it easier for the audience to sit through your talk.

but turns out in a way that reinforces it [(δ) in figure 2.1c], are, of course, the best.

3.6   Making Jokes

If you can amuse listeners occasionally with jokes, cartoons, or anecdotes, do it. Unfortunately, jokes are not easy to tell well, and an essential ingredient of the art is self-confidence, which requires time to develop. However, jokes or stories do not have to be very funny or very clever to help you connect with the audience. Keep them short and limit yourself to a few. You might open your talk by congratulating the winners of the Super Bowl the previous weekend or show empathy with your audience for suffering the tenth snowstorm of the season. Comments of this kind invariably go well. Private jokes do not. Avoid them. And do not invite the audience to address the hard questions to your absent coauthors or blame the latter for whatever mistakes remain in the paper. Such humor has worn thin. (By the way, when presenting joint work, always use *we*, no matter how strong the temptation to let listeners know that it was you who figured out the hard proof of Theorem 2.)

Cartoons or quotations are the easiest ways to bring out a smile because they don't require any particular skill in delivery. Just put them on a transparency. If your paper deals with networks, here is a suggestion I am certain will come off well: begin with the definition (it is always a good idea to start with definitions) of the term *network* by Samuel Johnson (1755): "Any thing reticulated, or decussated, at equal distances, with interstices between the intersections."

3.7   Being Flexible

As interactions with the audience may require you to depart from your intended plan, you should be ready to do so. Different audiences will react differently, and no two talks you give will follow exactly the same path. You need to be flexible enough to accommodate some of the wishes of your audience. But it is your presentation. You have structured it in particular ways to achieve certain objectives and are under no obligation to satisfy every whim of your audience. Even if someone asks you about it, you do not have to discuss an issue that is marginal to your work; nor should you give the details of a paper you mentioned as a background to your study that excited audience interest. (Maybe you made a mistake talking about it a little too enthusiastically, or perhaps a listener had heard about it and had long been eager to know more.) In some cases, you may give the audience a choice: are they interested in seeing an example of some phenomenon you are presenting, a table of numbers in an empirical study, or a sketch of a proof? But only present choices you know will not disturb your overall presentation. Don't offer to give a proof if it will take too long or is not central to your message.

If some part of the presentation has taken more or less time than you anticipated, you will need to adjust it to use the remaining time most efficiently. Anticipate these adjustments: have additional material ready to fill a gap, or plan what you could omit at various points without weakening your argument.

However, flexibility has its limits. Don't, for instance, change terminology and notation in the course of a talk. It is very difficult to do so. The chances are you will soon unconsciously return to the terms or variables you have been using for so many months. Therefore, even if someone suggests a change that seems like a good idea, acknowledge the help but don't implement it on the spot. Simply state that, for the time being, you will stick with your familiar language and notation.

3.8   Surprising Your Audience

Many speakers feel obligated to surprise their audience with counterintuitive results. In some fields, it seems to be a tradition. You will certainly make a name for yourself if you successfully challenge conventional wisdom; and the opposite strategy—emphasizing how much your results agree with common sense—will not have your listeners on the edge of their seats. However, there is danger in overemphasizing the element of surprise in your findings. When fully understood, nothing is really surprising. Moreover, your conclusions did not come out of thin air but out of your assumptions; it is likely that a number of them are simplifications or approximations you made for the sake of analytical convenience. By overselling the novelty of your conclusions, you are inviting the audience to ferret out which of the assumptions are responsible for them and to challenge your choice. This will force you to a defensive position. If you have not figured out the exact role of each assumption in bringing about the results, you will lose this little game that you unwittingly set up. (Remember, though, that one mark of a good study is the detailed knowledge you have about possible variants of your model.)

4   Interacting with the Audience

As mentioned above, interacting with your audience may mean being
flexible from time to time, and occasionally improvising. In this section
I discuss a number of ways you can strengthen these interactions and
make your presentation more effective.

4.1   Answering Questions

You are likely to encounter several types of questions and different kinds
of questions call for different kinds of answers. But before answering
any question, make sure you have fully understood it. If not, request
the person to restate or rephrase it.

- You can and should answer quickly requests for clarification of a point
  of language or notation.
- Questions revealing a misunderstanding of some technical or
  conceptual aspect of your paper are more difficult to answer.
  Answer them carefully and thoughtfully. You should expect some
  misunderstandings—and not just misunderstandings of the difficult
  parts of your paper. Treat everyone with respect, including someone
  who did not get a point that is obvious to you, or that you think
  should be obvious. Nothing is completely obvious to everyone. Before answering, think about what you may have said, or not said, to
  cause the confusion. Perhaps you forgot to give a crucial piece of information without which a point is not obvious—or perhaps not even
  true. Or the questioner may have been distracted when you gave
  that information; you cannot expect everyone to be with you all of
  the time.
- Repeated and irrelevant questions are harder to deal with. Avoid getting bogged down in addressing points made by someone who clearly
  is totally lost. Also, learn standard ways of dealing with counterproductive interruptions, for example: "That's a good point. Later I will
  give an example that will make it completely transparent" (if you have
  such an example), or "That's an interesting question (you do not have
  to mean it), but I would like to focus on a different one," or "I'd like
  to discuss this issue with you after the seminar." (In the latter case, do
  mean it. Don't leave the room without trying to catch the person who
  asked the question.)

- Questions that challenge your approach or your results are, of course, the hardest to deal with. Here, self-assured modesty is the best strategy. Don't oversell your claims but show that, given the state of the literature, your results constitute a worthwhile advance. Respond to critical questioning by stating your counterobjections as well as you can, but do not belabor your point in hopes that your opponent will acknowledge that you are right. That won't happen very often. Make your case and move on.

Right after your seminar, make note of questions you wished you had answered better, as well as of suggestions for improving your work. Occasionally, you can jot something down during the talk, though that is often a little awkward.

4.2   Choosing Pitch and Pace

A corollary of the observation that some people understand more slowly than others is that some people understand faster than others. Such discrepancies are particularly prevalent in job-market talks attended by departments at large, including people in fields completely different from yours. You will recognize who is ahead by their insightful questions, their nodding approval, and their references to relevant papers. These signs are particularly encouraging when you feel nervous. You will tend unconsciously to start directing your attention primarily at these people—looking in their direction, speaking at their level, and leaving the others behind. Try to avoid such behavior. Discreetly acknowledging the perceptiveness of a comment is certainly appropriate; and, occasionally, you may make a few technical observations for the benefit of those who have some prior knowledge of your subject. However, most of your presentation—and certainly your concluding comments—should be at a comfortable level of discussion for everyone in the room.

4.3   Bringing Attention (Back) to Yourself

If listeners start debating among themselves an issue that came up in your presentation and threatening to use up time you need, interrupt them—politely but firmly. Your host may take over to silence the debaters, but don't count on it. You have to take charge. (By the way, the best way to control your audience is to control your material.)

5 Transparencies

In the past ten or fifteen years, it has become standard to use transparencies for presenting one's work. They have a number of benefits, and some dangers too. I start with a list of their benefits and then give some advice on preparing and using them so as to avoid their pitfalls.

5.1 Benefits of Transparencies

- Show and tell is always better than just telling. Of course, that is just an argument against making long speeches and supports any kind of presentation involving visual aids. Information is indeed very effectively transmitted visually. Even if words convey the message clearly, visual aids can make it even clearer.

- Transparencies also save time during the presentation. When delivering a theory paper, there may be a rare (make that very rare) occasion when you want listeners to see a complicated equation or the sketch of an algebraic derivation. They won't, however, enjoy watching you write on the board. In this case, a transparency may be unavoidable. Do not, though, totally dismiss the idea of writing during a presentation. As I discuss later, the writing process, if well thought out, can be very informative.

  In an empirical paper, by the same token, you may have decided to show a table of data. Of course, you do not expect listeners to study it entry by entry. You merely want to comment on some of the numbers, or help them discover certain patterns. Present the simplest version of the table that allows you to do so. Entries need not include all the digits with which they are given in the sources where you encountered them, nor your table all the years of your time series. Distill the information and present it in the form of simple graphs. The main, perhaps the only, benefit of showing an entire table of data is that someone in the audience with a good eye for numbers may notice a pattern you had not seen, which might help you in future work.

  If you decide to show the table, you have several choices. One is to refer members of the audience to your printed paper. Another is to distribute a handout, prepared for the occasion. A third is to use transparencies. I prefer transparencies, even if the paper has been distributed or you brought handouts. Having everyone looking at the board, instead of individually looking down at a paper or a handout, is indeed more conducive to good communication. You can more easily attract people's joint attention to a crucial component of a formula or specific parts of a table by pointing at the screen, rather than by instructing them to find Definition 3 or Table 5 in the paper.

- Transparencies also relieve you from memorizing. You can achieve the same result by preparing notes, but transparencies are easier for you to read and they let the audience read along with you.

- They have a psychological benefit. Knowing that your entire presentation is right there in a written form instead of having to reproduce all of it on the board will boost your self-confidence.

- Transparencies will save you a lot of preparation time if you have to give the same talk several times. So would a good set of notes, of course. But be careful: if you rely too much on the transparencies you wrote for an earlier talk, you may not have the material as fresh in your mind as you would if you had to rehearse your points by writing them on the board. Practicing once more in your hotel room, or in the conference room before your session, will remind you of a difficulty you encountered on a previous occasion and how to best deal with it. If you do not prepare because you expect to find everything you need on your transparency, the same problem may come up again and you may not be ready to handle it. There is always a danger that you will forget some difficulty you had explaining a proof or a logical development. But turn the difficulty to your benefit; being forced to reconstruct an argument while preparing your talk may lead you to a new and better way of doing the proof.

In general, I am not fond of transparencies, and in attempting to articulate the reasons why, I admit that I mainly came up with reasons why I do not like them when not used well. However, no matter how good they are, an essential argument against them remains: transparencies deprive you of the dynamic structure of time that a good oral presentation can exploit and that a paper lacks. Showing step by step how logic inexorably takes us to a certain conclusion is what we try to do in the classroom; we continue to use blackboards there, in spite of the increasing availability and acceptability of overhead projectors, because we know that they are the best way to reach that goal. Transparencies never have the vividness of arguments constructed in front of an audience element by element. Progressively elaborating a theory on the board is certainly more work for the speaker, but unfortunately, when deciding whether to make it easy for themselves or easy for their audiences, speakers too often choose the former.

5.2 Preparing Transparencies

If you decide to use transparencies, here are a few do's and don't's about preparing them.

- Although the norm is to show printed text, I believe handwritten transparencies are more effective. In general, LATEX looks very good, but printed output is still not as eye-catching as a well-designed transparency done by hand. Certainly—except for that rare table of numbers you want the audience to contemplate in its entirety (see above)— never project entire pages of your paper, or paragraphs, or even complete sentences.

    If you do your transparencies by hand, write legibly, in sufficiently large letters. If your handwriting is not good, compensate by using block letters or capital letters. Exploit the freedom to vary size and shape to suggest structure and logic and to add emphasis. Underline critical assumptions in a theorem; circle important entries in a matrix; draw arrows between conditions to indicate how they relate; and, to show inclusions of sets, use Venn diagrams. You may argue that you can do most of these things with LATEX. True, but not as well. Consider the inventiveness of advertisers trying to get your attention in newspapers or on television. Their new low price is not simply underlined, or printed in a larger font; it is circled by hand, or surrounded by a large star, or made into a cartoon. The same freedom advertisers exercise in displaying their goods is available for academic presentations too. Any kind of information—historical, technical, or scientific—can be presented more effectively with the imaginative use of visual devices, as beautifully demonstrated by Edward Tufte (1983).

    Another option, adding handwriting to printed text, allows you to combine the professional look of LATEX output with the expository tricks I just mentioned.

- Use colors. Even if they have no functional significance, the mere visual stimulation they provide will capture audience attention. It is better to make one transparency red, the next one green, then back to red, and so on, than to do them all in black. Colors that indicate the structure of an argument are, of course, even better. You might for instance use one color for the assumptions and another one for the results. You can write in red a point you want listeners to be especially careful about. Using too many colors can be counterproductive, though: I have seen transparencies on which each category of objects—assumptions, definitions, propositions, theorems, and so on—had its own color. I was blinded, not dazzled.[2]

- Do not cram too much on each transparency. For printed text, enlargement is necessary (I suggest at least 24-point type). Make the margins wide enough to ensure that the edges of your text are not cut off and that most of it is readable at once. You shouldn't have to reposition the slide too many times as you comment on different parts of it. Depending on the configuration of the seminar room and the size of your audience, you probably will have to adjust each transparency at least once to show the bottom part of it; otherwise it will appear too low on the screen for people in the back of the room to see it.

- Do not write complete sentences, unless they are very short. "Equilibrium exists" and "Equilibrium is efficient" are good. "Under the assumptions of Section 1, an equilibrium may not exist, but under these assumptions efficiency of equilibrium is guaranteed" is bad. Lists and enumerations are better, because they help indicate structure. Compare these two formats:

THEOREM 1   Under the assumptions of continuity, convexity and monotonicity, an equilibrium exists and every equilibrium is efficient.

and

THEOREM 1

Continuity
Important for existence → **Convexity**   ⟹   **Equilibrium** *exists is efficient*
Monotonicity
Important for efficiency ↗

---

2. The functional use of colors was impressed upon me by a high school Latin teacher. To force us to uncover the grammatical structure of a text before we were permitted to attempt to translate it, he had us rewrite it in our notebooks in colors. I still remember them: black for principal clauses (white on the blackboard), red for relative clauses, blue for subordinate clauses, and green for absolute ablatives.

Write on one transparency the list of your criticisms of the earlier literature on the subject, on another, the list of assumptions on preferences; on a third, a list of applications of your model; and so on. Use the items on the list as prompts for discussion of the successive features of your paper. The items should not themselves be the discussion. Nor should the prompts contain the kind of abbreviations you use in your private notes. Abbreviations are acceptable only if is easy to guess what they mean.

Under what kinds of circumstances are transparencies particularly useful? Suppose, for example, that you want to describe an algorithm used to solve matching problems. You could write out the list of instructions with all the details. But it is much more effective to put the algorithm to work in an example. Construct the simplest preference profile that illustrates the various cases listed in the instruction manual of the algorithm. It would be pointless to try to memorize this profile and not instructive for the audience to watch you copy it onto the blackboard. Instead, display it on a transparency, with arrows indicating the first step of the algorithm and which agents are matched and leave. (You may actually draw the arrows as you speak.) Use the example to explain why these agents leave: that is, what are the general rules of the algorithm. That takes you to the second step. Show it on a second transparency, and so on.

As the above discussion suggests, a good transparency is probably not one that members of the audience can figure out without your help; it simply serves as a support for your explanation. You will help them understand the algorithm—and perhaps have fun in the process—because they see it at work. If the algorithm is complicated, you can show two or three examples of increasing complexity or some examples that cover different possible configurations of the parameters. By contrast, a list of formal instructions would be heavy in notation, encumbered with multiple subscripts to indicate agents and steps, and would provide only an abstract understanding of the algorithm. Nobody has ever learned to drive a car by reading a book about driving; the only way to learn is to get behind the wheel and drive around the block, and then along routes that are progressively richer in turns, intersections, and hazards.

• Divide your presentation into units. Devote one transparency, or a block of transparencies, to each unit. If a transparency is only two-thirds filled, leave it that way. If, instead, you begin a new unit there, then continue it on the next slide, you won't be able to conveniently change the order in which to present the elements of your paper, to omit a subject, or return to a point discussed earlier. Revisions will also be more work. This "modular" feature of transparencies is one of their important benefits.

- Number your transparencies discreetly in a corner (the audience does not have to see the numbers); or, give them short titles (the audience can see those). If you have to go back to a certain transparency to clarify a point someone is confused about, to remind the audience of some definition, or to compare a theorem to a previous one, it should be easy to find the earlier slide. Transparencies have the knack of getting out of order as soon as they are shown. Numbering or titling them will help you retrieve from the pile the ones you need. Alternatively, you can print two copies of a transparency you want to show twice. Separate transparencies by blank sheets. (Even when only two transparencies are sitting directly on top of each other, they are both impossible to read.)

- In addition to the transparencies you intend to use, prepare some concerning points that might come up. Keep these extras in a separate folder.

5.3 Using Transparencies

There are a number of tricks to using transparencies effectively. Here are a few of the most important.

- You can show the whole of a transparency right away or you can uncover each item it lists as you discuss it. Some listeners dislike having a speaker dispense the text line by line, not letting them see the next line or the next paragraph until the speaker decides they are ready for it. Perhaps they slightly resent the control exercised over them. Nonetheless, there are clear advantages to displaying the transparency progressively. It helps the audience stay focused on each point as it arises.

  But hiding part of a slide requires work that may distract you or the audience: repeatedly adjusting the cover forces you to go back and forth between the screen and the projector. (The cover often falls off the projector, which requires more trips.)

  If, on the other hand, you show the whole transparency at once, people have to decide whether to read it or listen to you explaining it. We cannot listen and read at the same time. You can show and tell only if you show a little, or tell a little. This is one reason why lists of discussion items are preferable to complete sentences: there is not that much to read, so the audience can listen too.

You can, of course, read the transparency aloud as listeners read it; but if you spend too much time reading to them, they will wish they had stayed home—where they can read faster, and more selectively.

• Do not look down at the transparency on the projector and point to the formula there. Instead, look and point at the screen. You should know exactly what audience members sees, and the only way you can do that is to look at the screen yourself. You cannot count on them to tell you that part of the transparency is not showing. They may not even realize that something relevant is missing; they may be waiting for you to adjust the transparency; or they may expect someone else to tell you or just be tired of repeatedly asking you to adjust the slide.

Is it impolite to turn your back to the audience to face the screen? Not at all. Orchestra conductors turn their back on the audience without offending. In both cases, there are good functional reasons for the behavior. Nonetheless, you should mostly look at the audience. If you don't, it is probably because you have too many transparencies or too much information on each one and the audience is spending too much time reading.

• An alternative strategy is to present the components of some argument on the board and then show a transparency in which they are assembled. Such a strategy combines the benefits of both means of exposition. You shouldn't, however, go back and forth between transparencies and the board too often, especially if the screen hides too much of the blackboard and you have to keep lowering and raising it. If you keep the screen down, you may have only two narrow strips of the board on either side of it to write on. If you choose to do that anyway and the screen is far from the wall, don't underestimate the extent of parallax.

5.4 Two Examples

In this subsection, I discuss two examples that illustrate a number of the points I have made so far about what to show and how to show it. First, consider how you might present the definition of the uniform rule, a rule designed to allocate a commodity among consumers having single-peaked preferences (Benassy, 1982). Here is the notation: N is the set of agents; for each $i \in N$, R_i is agent i's preference relation, with $p(R_i)$ designating the most preferred amount; Ω is the social amount of the good to distribute; X is the set of feasible allocations; $\mathcal{R}^N$ is the class of preference profiles. Finally, an economy is a pair $(R, \Omega) \in \mathcal{R}^N \times \mathbb{R}_+$.

A first option is to show on your transparency the definition as you would first write it, that is,

UNIFORM RULE, U The allocation $x \in X$ is the *uniform allocation* of $(R, \Omega) \in \mathcal{R}^N_{sp} \times \mathbb{R}_+$ if there is $\lambda \in \mathbb{R}_+$ such that (i) when $\sum p(R_i) \geq \Omega$, then for all $i \in N$, $x_i = \min\{p(R_i), \lambda\}$, and (ii) when $\sum p(R_i) \leq \Omega$, then for all $i \in N$, $x_i = \max\{p(R_i), \lambda\}$.

In this form, the definition is very hard to read. It is better to write it in a way that shows that there are two cases and that they are exactly parallel.

UNIFORM RULE, U The allocation $x \in X$ is the *uniform allocation* of $(R, \Omega) \in \mathcal{R}^N_{sp} \times \mathbb{R}_+$ if there is $\lambda \in \mathbb{R}_+$ such that

(i) when $\sum p(R_i) \geq \Omega$, then for all $i \in N$, $x_i = \min\{p(R_i), \lambda\}$, and

(ii) when $\sum p(R_i) \leq \Omega$, then for all $i \in N$, $x_i = \max\{p(R_i), \lambda\}$.

The next formulation is a little lighter, because I have discovered that certain words could be omitted and that so could the references to the domain of economies and to the set to which the generic agent belongs.

UNIFORM RULE, U $x = U(R, \Omega)$ if there is λ such that

(i) $\sum p(R_i) \geq \Omega$ implies that for all i, $x_i = \min\{p(R_i), \lambda\}$,

(ii) $\sum p(R_i) \leq \Omega$ implies that for all i, $x_i = \max\{p(R_i), \lambda\}$.

The next option is the one I prefer. It best brings out the parallelism between the two cases by skipping in Case ii the parts that are the same in Case i. There is less to read, and the definition ends up being easier to understand.

UNIFORM RULE: $x = U(R, \Omega)$ if there is λ such that

(i) $\sum p(R_i) \geq \Omega \Rightarrow$ for all i, $x_i = \min\{p(R_i), \lambda\}$

(ii) $\underline{\quad\quad} < - \Rightarrow \underline{\quad\quad}$, $x_i = \max\{\underline{\quad}, -\}$

It is even better to add to the algebraic definition a figure illustrating the origin of these *max* and *min* expressions: that is, that they come from each agent being giving the choice of the amount the agent prefers in a certain budget set. When the sum of the peak amounts is greater than the amount available, the budget set is a segment from 0 to some λ; when the inequality goes the other way, it is a half-line from some λ to ∞. Figure 2.2, accompanied by a verbal explanation as given in the caption, illustrates the rule in each of these two cases.

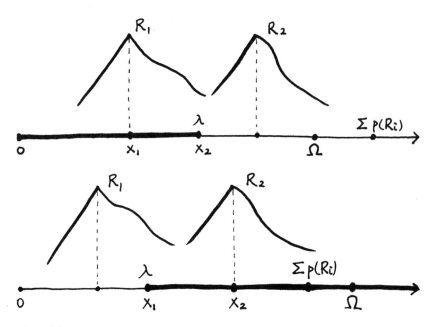

Figure 2.2
The Uniform Rule. Here (*pointing to the top diagram*), the sum of the preferred amounts is greater than the amount available. One can say that "there isn't enough" of the commodity. Then, pick a number λ and have each agent choose the amount the agent prefers subject to not exceeding the bound λ. The best choice for agent 1 in the interval $[0, \lambda]$ is his peak amount, which is the smaller of his peak amount and λ. For agent 2, the best choice is λ, which is also the smaller of her peak amount and λ. In general, this is what each agent i chooses, $\min\{p(R_i), \lambda\}$. Then, specify λ so that the sum of the best choices is equal to the social endowment of the commodity. There is a unique such λ, and the uniform allocation is the list of consumptions obtained then. Here (*pointing to the bottom diagram*), the amount to divide is greater than the sum of the peak amounts: one can say that "there is too much." This time, you impose a uniform lower bound on the agents' choices: each agent selects the preferred amount subject to consuming at least some λ you have picked. Agent 1 chooses λ—the larger of his peak amount and λ—and agent 2 chooses her peak amount—also the larger of her peak amount and λ. In general, this is what each agent i picks, $\max\{p(R_i), \lambda\}$. Then specify λ so as to achieve feasibility.

My second example is an algorithm to allocate indivisible goods. An economy here is defined as follows: N is the set of agents; each agent $i \in N$ owns one object, called object i; and is equipped with a preference relation R_i defined over the set of objects.

GALE'S ALGORITHM (Shapley and Scarf, 1974) For each agent $i \in N$, determine the object the agent prefers. If there is a cycle of agents, $i_1, i_2, \ldots, i_k$, such that for each $\ell \in \{1, \ldots, k\}$ (mod k), agent i_ℓ prefers the object owned by agent $i_{\ell+1}$ to any other object (for all $j \in N$, $O_{i_{\ell+1}} R_{i_\ell} O_j$), attribute to each agent in the cycle the object the agent prefers. Then, all agents in the cycles leave and the process is repeated with the remaining agents.

A better alternative is to substitute an example showing how to operate the algorithm (figure 2.3).[3] You would accompany the figure with the verbal explanation shown in the caption.

6 Proofs?

Should you give complete proofs of your results in an oral presentation? I would hardly ever recommend it. But do show parts of some proofs, to give the audience a sense of them, or demonstrate a proof in simple cases.

- The time needed to work out some of the basic properties of a model unfamiliar to your audience—before turning to your own contribution—is always well spent. Understanding the mechanics of the model well will make it easier for the audience to follow the innovations of your work. You might want to start, for instance, by explaining the simpler class of situations analyzed by an earlier author.

- As you introduce your own results, sketch some steps for some proofs. Presenting a complete proof is rarely feasible, however. Even a simple argument explained at the level of detail journals demand would consume too much time. Do it only if you need to draw an important lesson from the exercise.

- Instead, provide some insight into the logic underlying some of the proofs, what we call the *intuition* of the proofs. For the most important results, this is essential. A well-chosen special case will often suffice. By *well-chosen* I mean one that contains all the critical elements of the proof. A so-called intuition for a result that holds

---

3. At the second step of the algorithm, you may cross out on the transparency the objects that have disappeared.

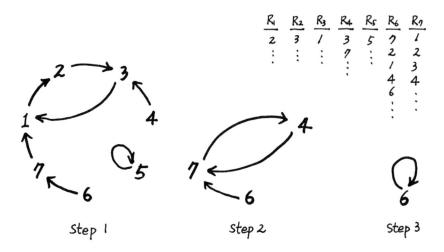

R_1	R_2	R_3	R_4	R_5	R_6	R_7
2	3	1	3	5	7	1
⋮	⋮	⋮	7	⋮	2	2
			⋮		1	3
					4	4
					6	⋮
					⋮	⋮

Step 1   Step 2   Step 3

Figure 2.3
Gale's Algorithm. The table shows agents' preferences. For instance, for agent 6, object 7 is the most desirable; object 2 is the second most desirable, and so on. At Step 1 of the algorithm, agents point to the particular object they each find most desirable: Agent 1 points to object 2. Agent 5 points to himself because the object he owns is the one he prefers, and so on. There are two cycles: one involving agents 1, 2 and 3, and a degenerate cycle involving only agent 5. Allocate objects along the cycles: that is, give object 2 to agent 1, object 3 to agent 2, and object 1 to agent 3; also let agent 5 keep the object he owns. Then let the agents in the cycles leave with their objects. At Step 2, the remaining agents point to the one of the remaining objects that each prefers. Agent 4 now points to object 7, which, as you can see from the preference table, happens to be her second-most desirable object in the entire initial list; agent 6 also again points to object 7, which is still present; and agent 7 now points to object 4, which is way down on his list, because the three objects he prefers to object 4 are gone. At Step 2, there is one cycle, which involves agents 4 and 7. Allocate objects along the cycle and let these two agents leave. At Step 3, there is only one agent left—agent 6—and, of course, she has to point to herself. She keeps her object.

only under a certain restriction on preferences not imposed in earlier literature—or for a certain choice of quantification that differs from the standard formulation—is not useful if that restriction or quantification is not mentioned. How could that possibly be the intuition for the proof? Informal explanations intended to help an audience grasp some complicated development can be more difficult to understand than the complete argument itself when the well-intentioned speaker leaves out certain quantifications or merely suggests definitions without stating them in adequate detail.

• If you do decide to show a proof, present it in the simplest way that still demonstrates its essential structure. Here is an illustration.

In principle, to show by induction that statement $P(k)$ holds for $k = 0, 1, \ldots$, it suffices to establish it for the base case (when $k = 0$), and then to show that if it holds up to k, then it holds for $k + 1$. That is not, however, what you should do. The proof for the base case is often quite different from the proof for the general case and, although sometimes considerably simpler, is not very informative. On the other hand, the proof of how to pass from k to $k + 1$ is frequently notationally complex and opaque. My advice is simply to show how to pass from the base case to $k = 1$. If you have enough time, and if it is important for the audience to understand the proof, also show how to pass from $k = 1$ to $k = 2$. If you have even more time, you can show the base case as well. Whatever you do, skip the general case, with its messy generic subscripts and superscripts.

To avoid getting bogged down in details, it is sometimes acceptable to omit from a proof certain conditions without which it is in fact not correct. For instance, you may give an explanation in terms of marginal rates of substitution without having discussed the issue of smoothness of preferences. Or your proof may not be valid on the boundary of the consumption space—though you need not mention it. There is a little deception here, but it is for a good cause. Almost everyone would support you for not raising a peripheral issue so that you can keep the focus on the central point. Another, and perhaps slightly safer, way to proceed is to warn listeners that your explanation does not quite cover all cases. Again, you do not have to be specific about which cases are not covered.

7 Writing on the Board

At the board, there are a number of useful tricks to minimize the amount of writing you do and to make the writing process itself informative. Some are effective for almost any subject, while for your particular area you will have to devise your own special tricks.

7.1 Restrict Yourself to a Few Colors

Writing on the board in different colors is nice, but the rule enunciated for transparencies applies here as well; don't use too many colors. You may confuse your audience. Besides, markers dry out if you don't put the caps back on, and constantly changing colors and dealing with the caps is distracting—to you and your listeners.

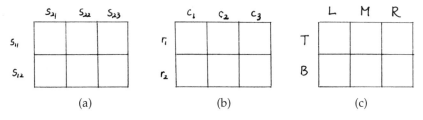

Figure 2.4
Three Ways of Labeling Strategies. (a) The strategies' generic labels do not reflect the structure of the game. (b) The labels are better here because they suggest the kinds of object that the strategies are: rows or columns. (c) This choice is best because strategy names are very precisely tailored to the objects they designate: Top and Bottom for the row player; Left, Middle, and Right for the column player.

7.2   Use as Little Notation as Possible

It is often useful to name some—though not all—of the variables you talk about in order to eliminate ambiguities. But there are means other than introducing notation to be unambiguous. For instance, if you are illustrating an issue involving preferences by means of diagrams, draw one preference map in green and the other in blue and refer to their owners as green and blue agents. Here are two additional examples. Compare the following three sentences pertaining to the game described in Figure 2.4:

1. If player 1, the row player, plays s_{11}, player 2, who is the column player, should play s_{21} (2.4a).

2. If the row player plays the first row, the column player should play the middle column (2.4b).

3. If Row plays Top, Column should play Middle (2.4c).

The last sentence is undoubtedly best. Now, which of the following two statements is better?

1. Agent 1, who has Cobb-Douglas preferences, when maximizing over the budget set that results when the price of good 1 is relatively higher ...

2. The Cobb-Douglas agent, when maximizing over the relatively steeper budget line ...

7.3   *Write Formulas from the Inside Out*

Although most of you learned to read and write from left to right, it is better to create formulas in stages, in a way that reveals their structure. Often, that means starting from the inside.

The following example illustrates this logic. Let N be a set of agents, $\mathcal{R}$ a set of possible preference relations defined over some alternative space Z, and $\varphi: \mathcal{R}^N \to Z$ a correspondence. Suppose that you want to explain what it means for "the game form (S, h), consisting of the profile of strategy spaces $S = (S_i)_{i \in N}$ and outcome function $h: S \to Z$, to implement the correspondence φ in Nash equilibria." For each preference profile $R \in \mathcal{R}^N$ the set of Nash equilibrium allocations of the game form (S, h) when played by agents with preferences R—let us denote this set $E(S, h, R)$—coincides with the set of allocations that the solution would select for R, namely $\varphi(R)$. You could write this, from left to right, as:

$$\text{For all } R \in \mathcal{R}^N, h(E(S, h, R)) = \varphi(R).$$

But there is a better way—one that illustrates how the sentence is built up. First, write down the game form (S, h). Explain that you cannot study its equilibria until you have the preference profile R. Then erase the right parenthesis to make room for R. You now have the game (S, h, R). Take the opportunity to emphasize the difference between a game and a game form. Add the letter E in front of the expression to indicate that you will calculate the equilibria of the game (S, h, R): this gives you the set $E(S, h, R)$. Next, apply the outcome function h to it to obtain the corresponding set of equilibrium allocations. To the right of the resulting expression, first write down the preference profile R, then apply the solution φ to it. Next, insert the equality sign between the two sets. Finally, add the quantification to indicate that this equality should hold for every preference profile in the domain.

Line by line, the expression would successively appear as

$$(S, h)$$
$$(S, h$$
$$(S, h, R)$$
$$E(S, h, R)$$
$$h(E(S, h, R))$$
$$h(E(S, h, R)) \quad \varphi(R)$$
$$h(E(S, h, R)) = \varphi(R)$$
$$\text{For all } R \in \mathcal{R}^N, h(E(S, h, R)) = \varphi(R).$$

Earlier I referred to the dynamic aspect of oral presentations. The ability to sequence at will the components of definitions in this way is certainly one of their major benefits.

7.4 *Watch Your Subscripts and Superscripts*

If you add a subscript and superscript to each variable as you write it, you will almost certainly get confused, and end up writing a superscript instead of a subscript, or vice versa.

There are ways to avoid errors of this kind. One, of course, is to eliminate double indices altogether. If you insist on using both, my advice is to write them more slowly than you write the rest of the formula. It also helps to use double subscripts or double superscripts instead of combinations. But combinations are often clearer in a written text, and you probably want your oral presentation to match the written text in that respect. If you decide to combine them—say by using subscripts for goods and superscripts for agents—proceed by rows. First write a row of as many copies of the variable as you need without any ornamentation; on a second pass add the subscripts, and on the last pass, decorate with the superscripts. Alternatively, write the variables and subscripts on the first pass and the superscripts on the second pass.

7.5 *Use Common Formats*

It is often easier on a board than in a paper to format definitions or results to bring out their relationships. Write them one below the other and only repeat the parts that are different. If, to return to an example I presented in Chapter 1, you first show that

LEMMA 1 $A, B,$ and $C \Longrightarrow D$.

and your second result differs from the first one in that B is replaced by B' and D by D', write it as

LEMMA 2 $—, B',$ and $— \Longrightarrow D'$.

and not as

LEMMA 2 $A, B',$ and $C \Longrightarrow D'$.

You will save writing time, and the audience will save reading time. Indeed, it will be immediately evident that the two theorems differ in the second assumption and in the conclusion. That is the only thing the audience will read; in fact, there is nothing else to read.

7.6   Divide for Emphasis

If you have proved that under certain assumptions there is a unique equilibrium, that is how you will often write up the result, in that compact way. When you explain the result, however, it may be more useful to point out that it actually consists of two statements: "An equilibrium exists" and "There is no more than one equilibrium."

Similarly, if you have shown the equality between the two sets A and B, you can state your result cleanly as $A = B$. In a seminar, though, you may want to state and explain separately that $A \subseteq B$ and $A \supseteq B$.

8   Conclusion

To explain something really well, you need to know a good deal more than that limited set of facts. The more you know in addition to what you explain, the better your explanation will be. Using the image of an iceberg, which, in the popular-science cliché, is nine-tenths submerged, what you show should only be a small part of what you know. Some of the questions your audience asks will probably pertain to aspects of your problem you did not bring up. You have to be ready to talk about them. The more thoroughly you are able to discuss issues peripheral to your paper, the more you will impress your audience. And the more interested they are, the more feedback you will get and the more stimulating your presentation will be for everyone, including you.

When they leave the seminar room, all members of the audience should be able to state your main message. Can they? If the answer is yes, your talk has already achieved an important objective.

9   References

Bénassy, Jean-Pascal. *The Economics of Market Disequilibrium.* New York: Academic Press, 1982.

Jackson, Matthew, "Notes on Presenting a Paper." Mimeographed paper. California Institute of Technology, 1998.

Johnson, Samuel. *A Dictionary of the English Language.* London, 1755.

Shapley, Lloyd S., and Herbert Scarf. "On Cores and Indivisibility." *Journal of Mathematical Economics* 1 (1974): 23–37.

Tufte, Edward. *The Visual Display of Quantitative Information.* Cheshire, Conn: Graphics Press, 1983.

3   Writing Referee Reports

You may have been asked by your adviser or another faculty member in your department to referee a paper for a journal. You agonized over the job, not knowing exactly what was expected of you. As a young assistant professor and scholar you are also very likely to receive other requests to review manuscripts submitted for journal or book publication. It is not, however, a skill taught in any of the classes you took. Even if you have already submitted one of your own papers to a journal and received reports on it, they probably will provide you a very incomplete guide. The purpose of this chapter, therefore, is to help you evaluate others' work and produce a useful critique. Your two main goals will be to assess the manuscript's suitability for publication and advise the author about improving his or her work.[1]

1   Components of a Report

Your report should consist of the following components, listed here in order of increasing specificity and decreasing importance. They pertain first to the substance of the contribution and then the quality of its exposition.

1. Summary of the paper
2. Overall evaluation of the paper with your recommendation about the publication decision
3. Comments about the model and the results

---

1. Hamermesh (1992) concludes his useful article about getting one's own work published with some good advice on refereeing. You will, of course, have other occasions to evaluate others' work. Eckel (1999) provides very useful guidance on reviewing grant proposals. I suggest that you read her essay not only when writing such a report but also when drafting your own proposals.

4. Assessment of the exposition
   a. The structure of the paper
   b. Secondary aspects of the exposition
   c. Details of presentation

I take up each of these items in the following subsections.

1.1 *Summary*

I recommend beginning your report with a summary of the article even though, as an associate editor or as an author, I have rarely found such summaries useful. Indeed, they often amount to little more than a restatement of the abstract and tend to be used to pad out reports. However, if the summary is *written in your own words* (instead of being lifted from the paper), it can be helpful in several ways.

- It makes the report a self-contained document—that is, one that can be read on its own.

- It reassures the associate editor and, then, the author that you have read and understood the paper.

- The effort required to describe the paper—I repeat *in your own words*—will be useful to you in forming your opinion. Summarizing will help you understand the nature of the author's contribution better. In the process, you may discover that you disagree with the author's view of certain aspects of the work and want to recommend highlighting the significance of a particular assumption or providing a different interpretation of the findings. If so, you are no longer summarizing the work and should make that clear, perhaps saying something like: "Although the author presents this paper as a contribution to the theory of strategic games, in my view the main result is Theorem 2, which has important implications for the theory of implementation. I suggest that the author present the study as a contribution to that literature."

1.2 *Overall Evaluation*

Your overall evaluation of the paper should be based on an assessment of the following points:

- Its significance for the field,

- Its appropriateness for the particular journal to which it has been submitted.

One criterion is the paper's originality: Is the contribution to the literature substantial enough? Another is subject matter: Is the topic pertinent to the journal's statement of purpose? (There should be a good match between them.)

Your evaluation should conclude with a recommendation about publication. Your advice can be one of the following:

- Publish it; and, if the journal has a notes section, recommend whether the paper should be a regular article or a note;
- Encourage the author to resubmit, reserving your opinion about publication until the author has addressed the points that concern you;
- Reject it.

Even if your recommend publication, you will undoubtedly have comments and suggestions for improvements, and you may feel that some changes are necessary. *Be explicit about which ones you see as essential.*

If you favor inviting resubmission, again, *be explicit about the improvements you require to endorse publication.* But be realistic. Don't accept the paper on condition that the author accomplish some unlikely feat of generalization. If acceptance would require too much improvement, it is safer to recommend rejection. Being vague or unreasonably demanding in your requests will put you in an awkward position in the second round, when you will recognize that you were not precise enough or were asking for more than could reasonably be delivered; you will then have to decide whether the improvements go far enough in the direction you indicated to justify publication. You also complicate the associate editor's task, making it harder to argue the case for rejection should the editor decide that the paper has not passed the threshold for acceptance.

1.3   Comments on Model and Results

You should reflect on the interest of the model and the significance of the results. Are the reasons for undertaking the study compelling? Is the model specified so as to capture the essential aspects of the phenomenon the author is attempting to explain? Are the assumptions economically relevant and the conclusions interesting?

You should also think about the mathematics used. Are the results correct as stated? Could they be strengthened? Could their proofs be simplified? Why did the author rely on sophisticated techniques when all earlier studies used elementary mathematics? Is the data used to prove the thesis well chosen for that purpose? Have the appropriate significance tests been run?

You should not necessarily expect to find the answers to all possible questions of this sort, but if the paper does not contain the information needed to clarify most of them, request that the author provide it at the next round—either in the reply to the referees or in the paper itself. You may end up deciding that some of the material in the reply is worth including in the paper or, conversely, that some developments inserted in the revision in response to your comments do not deserve to be published after all. As time passes, your thinking may evolve, or the revision may contain information that requires you to modify the opinion expressed on the original version. Be flexible and, certainly, acknowledge any misconceptions you may have had during the first round.

If you think the paper is fundamentally flawed, you will find it difficult to motivate yourself to work through the proofs and you are not obliged to do so in such a case. On the other hand, you should have checked the proofs of a paper that you recommend for publication. Occasionally, this process takes considerable time, and it may be acceptable, even unavoidable, to skip some of it. Since a proof often includes several steps or cases with similar structures, you may look at only one of them at your first reading. If you find too many imperfections in the proofs you study in detail (missing quantifications, inequalities going the wrong way, and so on), you will grow suspicious of the entire work. You won't trust the author about the steps left to the reader with the claim that they are "easy" or "similar to proofs in an earlier paper" or "only involved tedious calculations" (the standard excuses). Insist that in addition to fixing all the errors you noted, the author provide complete arguments, either in the revision or in a reply to the referee. Reserve your judgment until then. If the author has stumbled too often, simply reject the paper.

If you have discovered no flaws in the proofs that you did check, you will feel reasonably confident that the argument is correct as a whole, especially if it makes intuitive sense. Under these circumstances, you may be justified in omitting some proofs or some steps of proofs. If you do, though, inform the associate editor of how extensively you have checked the mathematics.

1.4   Comments on the Exposition

The author should have done everything possible to make the study as transparent as possible. But it is not sufficient that the exposition be clear. You should ask whether it could be even clearer. Nor is it sufficient that the paper be understandable by researchers in the same field. If it can be written so as to be accessible to a wider audience without any loss of substance, that is what the author should do.

It will help you formulate your comments to think about papers you found particularly lucid or enjoyable and identify the reasons why you felt that way.

A natural way to organize your comments on the quality of the exposition is to start with issues of overall structure and proceed to questions of details.

- *Comments about the structure of the paper.* The structure of the work should be immediately clear. It is the frame that supports the whole thing. Ask yourself whether the paper is well organized. Is the progression from introduction to conclusion natural? Is this issue really central to the argument? Should this proof be relegated to an appendix? Would it be more effective to present this theorem as a lemma instead and this proposition as a corollary of the main theorem?

- *Comments about secondary aspects of the exposition.* Address whether a step in a proof taken from some earlier article needs to be reproduced or whether a reference to the work suffices. Would numerical examples or figures be useful? Should more effort be devoted to placing the paper in the context of the literature on the topic?

  Problems that are not serious for you because you know the literature may in fact prevent others from understanding anything. You may read an ambiguous quantification as it was intended, but readers not familiar with the relevant literature might read it the wrong way; and for them the paper may make no sense. Make sure that every detail is handled correctly.

  Although the general inclination of referees is to ask for deletions, do not hesitate to ask for changes that may lengthen the paper if you feel they will make it easier to understand, even though they do not lead to more general results. If you recommend shortening the paper, be, once again, very precise; authors are always reluctant to eliminate anything. A request to reduce the length by half is not precise enough: list the specific cuts. And when evaluating the revision, don't be fooled by changes in font size, margins, or spacing that give the appearance of compliance but don't actually shorten the work.

- *Comments about the details of the presentation.* Tell the author whether a formula should be displayed on a separate line or a condition given a different name. Should the importance of a conclusion be emphasized by using a distinctive typeface (such as italics)? Should two paragraphs be merged? You may also add a list of the typographical errors you noticed.

2   Distinguish between Nonnegotiable Requests and Suggestions for Changes

You may want to divide your requests for revisions into two parts.

- Some requests for changes are nonnegotiable: The model should be coherent; there should be no errors in proofs; proper credit should be given to previous contributors. You have a right to demand that the author respect such universal principles of good writing as simplicity and unity. The structure of the paper should be clear and its language should be free of unnecessary technical jargon.

  In the revision, do not accept as an excuse for persisting in errors you pointed out, or in features of the paper to which you objected, that they are present, even common, in the earlier literature on the subject or in the work of such and such a well-known predecessor. We may temporarily accept the limitations of a model or of an approach because certain conceptual issues have not yet been satisfactorily resolved in the field, or because the right techniques have not been developed. That is a necessary precondition to progress. But committing errors that can be avoided, given the state of the art, hampers progress and is unacceptable.

- Other suggestions for change are simply ideas for the author to think about. You leave them to the discretion of the author. You believe that they would improve the paper, but you also see why the author might disagree. You are aware of counterarguments to your proposals or of the costs of implementing them. An additional way of justifying the model's specification may lengthen an already-long introduction; presenting a proof for the n-person case instead of the two-person case may obscure an argument that is now very transparent; dropping certain regularity assumptions on preferences and technologies may prevent the use of elementary mathematical tools; and so on.

Certain features of a paper may not be to your taste and yet be quite legitimate. In these cases you can only suggest changes and try to convince the author of your reasons for wanting them; you cannot insist on them. For instance, you may not care for the style in which the paper is written, but you can't force your own style on the author. You may have to accept a verbal or informal presentation of a proof if the author's goal is to make the argument easily accessible to the less mathematically oriented readers, even if your own preference is for a formal proof. However, suppose that this verbal proof is missing critical information, for example, that in an informal argument intended to provide the intuition of a proof, definitions are ambiguous or quantifications are not clear or no reference is made to a conceptually important assumption without which the formal proof would irrevocably fail. Then readers can only be fooled into believing that they understand the argument, and you should demand that these important elements be made explicit.

It is probably best to append your requests for changes to each part of your report as enumerated in the preceding section.

3   Evaluating Revisions

How do you go about assessing a revision? First, compare it to the earlier version, section by section and paragraph by paragraph. Check how each of your numbered recommendations and requests for changes has been implemented. If the paper has been significantly reorganized and the pagination changed, this will not be an easy exercise. In this case, an author's reply to the referees will be very helpful in guiding you through the changes. Request such a reply; authors rarely spontaneously supply one. If you asked for one and the author did not bother to send it, have the associate editor demand compliance. If the author has paid only lip service to your suggestions, write to the associate editor and point out the critical comments the author has ignored. Here, too, it is quite reasonable to request that the author comply before you study the paper.

Unless the changes are very minor, you need to go over the whole thing again. New errors are often made in the process of correcting existing ones. Some notational conflicts may appear; or the sequencing of definitions and results may be disturbed in ways that have escaped the author. Besides, several months have probably passed, and you may have new points to make.

Unless only a few problems remain, ask for another round of revisions.

4   Length and Style of the Report

I do not have a specific recommendation on how long your report should be. A review of a paper that suffers from a fundamental flaw may be very short, whereas comments on a paper you found exciting may take several pages. In that case, your assessment will probably be short, while your suggestions will constitute the bulk of the report.

Nor do I have a particular recommendation on the related question of how many hours you should devote to the job: the time needed will vary considerably from paper to paper. An hour may suffice for one that is obviously below the line for acceptance, whereas you may need four to five hours for a potentially publishable piece for which you have to supply a long list of requests and suggestions for changes. A paper with long or difficult proofs may take fifteen to twenty hours if it appears to be an important contribution that you think will be very critical for you to understand well for your own research. In this last case, strictly speaking, most of the time you spend will not be required to do the actual report.

Concerning the style of your report, my most important practical recommendation is to *number the various recommendations and requests that you make*. Don't lump several points together. If your request has two parts, call them Part 1 and Part 2. At the next round, the numbering will make it very easy to check out whether your suggestions have been taken into account. Sooner or later—and in fact sooner rather than later—you will receive a revision from an uncooperative author who has done the bare minimum to address your comments while claiming to deal with them thoroughly. By being precise in your demands, you will make it more difficult for authors to avoid making the changes you think are needed.

Referees' reports are not intended for publication, so do not bother polishing your English. Do not worry about stylistic issues such as repetitions, inconsistencies of tense, and so on, which can be time-consuming to correct. Save the effort for your own papers. Your priority is to be clear and definite. By revising your report to achieve these goals, you will eliminate most of the stylistic problems anyway.

5   The Cover Letter

Do you need a cover letter to the associate editor (apart from "Please find enclosed my report on so-and-so's paper. Sincerely")? Sometimes yes. A first (but rare) reason is that you may want to discuss concerns about a possible conflict of interest with your own work. Again, as discussed later, if you feel sufficiently strongly that there is such a conflict, you should decline the job at the outset.

Another reason is that you have harsh things to say and you fear being identified. The difficulty of remaining anonymous is all the greater if you need to mention work of your own that the author has failed to take into account properly. Such situations are, of course, not rare, and they will become more and more frequent as your CV lengthens. As noted earlier, in many cases, the associate editor has called on you to referee a paper because you have contributed to the relevant literature. Keep in mind, though, that complete anonymity is impossible anyway and that one of the first things some authors try to do when receiving a report is to figure out who wrote it.[2] It is something that you just have to accept.

If some issue of integrity, such as plagiarism, has to be raised, the cover letter may be where you should do so. On these occasions, however, it might be a good idea to first seek the advice of your adviser, if you still are a graduate student, or of one of your senior colleagues, if you are a young assistant professor.

Your overall assessment of the paper and your recommendation do not, however, belong in the cover letter. You may want to provide a short summary of your report, or restate there in a different way certain points that you make in the report. But I object to the explicit requests of some editors and to the policy of some journals that the recommendation about acceptance or rejection *not* appear in the report sent to the author but only in the cover letter.[3] When a paper is turned down, the author is entitled to know the basis on which the decision was made.

If you have not received an acknowledgment a few weeks after you sent your report, you may want to check with the associate editor that it was not lost in the mail—or in cyberspace.

6   General Recommendations

In this section, I discuss the need to take a critical stance and the extent of your responsibility to the journal and the author.

---

2. One clue: the person most frequently cited in the report is usually the author of the report.

3. I have heard several reasons for this policy. One is that it allows referees to feel more comfortable expressing negative opinions—it protects them. A second is that it shields authors from the harsh things a referee may have to say. The editor's letter can tone down overly critical comments made by referees.

6.1 *Expressing Judgment*

Like many first-time referees, you may not feel confident about expressing subjective opinions on the suitability for publication of someone else's work. Nonetheless, you should not limit yourself to an enumeration of objective statements about the paper. Take a stance. The following points should help you do that.

First, the associate editor will also look at the paper—and in some cases study it—and there may be other referees (although often there are not).

Moreover, subjective judgment is an inevitable part of the evaluation process. Some referees, perhaps feeling uncomfortable about rejecting a paper for subjective reasons, end up making poorly substantiated arguments against objective features of the paper in order to support a negative recommendation. For example, they emphasize errors in a proof when its imperfections could be fixed. (Errors are rarely completely avoided, and in some cases they do invalidate a proof.) Or they assert that the author's result is a special case of someone else's earlier theorem, when it is not (although it may well be closely related to a known theorem). Altogether, such referees are seriously undermining the usefulness of their reports. If you believe that the paper is not significant enough for the journal, express that judgment as the reason for your advice to reject it. Imperfections in proofs do not necessarily disqualify a paper from eventual publication. If the results appear to be true and are interesting, simply point out these imperfections and ask that they be eliminated. Also, if the relation between the results reported in the paper and other studies is unclear, demand that it be clarified. By itself, the fact that the author may not have understood this relation well, or may not have described it accurately, is not sufficient grounds for rejection.

What is very helpful to the associate editor, however, is for you to separate the statements of fact in your report from your expressions of judgment. Here is an illustration.

The theorem as written is incorrect. It would be correct, however, if preferences were required to be strictly convex." [Here you are making a comment about an objective aspect of the paper whose validity is not a matter of judgment.] Unfortunately, when strict convexity is imposed, the enlargement of the class of economies for which the author shows existence of equilibria is not of sufficient interest to justify publication in this journal. [Now you are expressing your subjective judgment, with which other readers may disagree.]

6.2 When Is Withholding Judgment Appropriate?

In some cases, the decision to publish or not will seem to be primarily a matter of general editorial policy. For instance, the paper is much longer than the articles commonly published in the journal. Or it deals with a subject that does not match well the journal's statement of purpose. Or it is written at a significantly higher or lower technical level than that of the journal's standard article. Perhaps it is more didactic in tone or purpose, or its contribution is principally conceptual, whereas the journal's emphasis is on techniques. Or vice versa. If so, raise these issues in your report and let the associate editor and the editor decide how to deal with them. In principle, they have sent you the paper because they do not object to considering it for their journal. But they may not, in fact, have looked at it in great detail.

6.3 The Referee's Responsibilities to the Journal and to the Author

Your main responsibility is to help the journal decide whether or not to publish the paper. But you should also consider helping the author produce a better article. You can usually do that at a small cost because you have thought a lot about the article.

Be generous with your advice. Even if you recommend rejection, your comments will help the author revise the paper for a different journal. Moreover, the other referees, and perhaps the associate editor, may disagree with you and favor publication; in that case, your comments will be helpful for this journal as well. Almost every paper contains something useful and publishable if properly reformulated and targeted to the right audience. Even if you feel sure the paper does not deserve to be published in the journal you are evaluating it for, why not let the author benefit from the efforts you expended in forming your opinion? Give your advice about the best means of bringing out its strong points for resubmission to a different journal. After all, you are probably one of the first readers (sometimes the only one) who has studied the paper so carefully. Admittedly, in some circumstances, it is difficult to motivate oneself to suggest improvements, especially when the author's objective seems to have been to violate all the standards of scholarship. (It does occur.)

Being generous with your advice, however, does not mean correcting major flaws in the author's logic or providing the proof of a conjecture stated in the paper. Although some of your comments might lead to major improvements, it is not your responsibility to produce such help. You are not a coauthor.

Conversely, very few papers are acceptable as originally submitted. Be tough. You do a disservice to the journal, and to the field (remember that it is in most cases your own field), by being too lenient. And you are not doing the author any favor by failing to mention all the problems you noticed. Moreover, it is easier if you are a little tougher than needed at the first round and slightly more permissive at subsequent rounds. After being too lenient on the first round you may discover in the revision issues you missed earlier that definitely have to be addressed before you can recommend publication.

Being tough is not the same as being mean. There is no pleasant way to tell an author that his or her work should be rejected, but that is absolutely no reason to be insulting. Do not make disparaging comments about the author's intelligence.

I have heard the argument that because in most cases a paper could be submitted to other journals, we need not worry too much about rejections that should have been acceptances. Certainly, we all make mistakes. Yet the argument comes dangerously close to condoning sloppy evaluations. Moreover, it is not really very convincing, given the hierarchical perceptions of different journals' prestige. In some areas, there are no more than three or four possible outlets for a given work, and they are rarely equivalent in terms of the visibility and status they would give the work or its author. Moreover, if you are the only referee for a paper, your opinion may carry a lot of weight. Finally, the author may have already submitted the paper two or three times. For a young person being considered for a promotion, an additional acceptance by a prestigious journal can be critical.

Yet one more point: if you happen to meet the author in person, there is no need to mention that you were the referee. It goes without saying that you will rarely be tempted to do so if you recommended rejection. But if you wrote a positive report, you might. The only reason for revealing your identity in a personal conversation is the desire to ingratiate yourself. Don't.

7   Deciding Whether to Accept a Refereeing Job

Now that you know what is expected of you when you receive a paper to referee, you may wonder whether you should accept the job. In general you should. But there are several reasons why you may decline.

- *You lack the expertise or the interest needed for the assignment.* Perhaps the associate editor has misjudged your area of specialization, and the subject of the paper is too far removed from what you know well. Refereeing a paper on a topic with which you are not familiar is a good opportunity to learn about a new area and you should consider seizing it, but be realistic. If the background reading necessary for you to properly evaluate the work is too extensive, you may not be able to gain the perspective on the subject required for a good report.

  Similarly, you should have some minimal interest in the literature to which the paper contributes. If you don't, you will find it difficult to motivate yourself to do the work, and your view of the field will be unfairly reflected in your opinion.

- *You fear a conflict of interest.* That is another good reason to turn down a refereeing job. Conflict may arise for various reasons. You may be currently engaged in similar research and feel proprietary about the subject, or even about some specific results contained in the paper. Or you have had an article on the same topic rejected, which you think might make it difficult not to overreact in judging others' work. If you are concerned that your emotions will get in the way of a fair evaluation, decline the job.

- *You have previously evaluated the paper for another journal.*[4] To the extent that submission to a second journal is comparable to an appeal in the judicial system, it is crucial to a fair hearing to have a new judge. In most cases, there will be other competent people to evaluate the paper, and its fate should not be made to hinge on the taste of a single person.

  However, there are also good reasons why you may want to look at the paper again and send a report.

  - It has been revised, perhaps substantially.[5]
  - Your opinion of the paper, or perhaps the field, has evolved.
  - The second journal differs significantly in style and reputation from the first.
    (In these cases, a different sort of report is called for. You cannot simply pull out the old one.)

---

4. This will not, of course, happen for a while.
5. You will also receive resubmissions in which none of the comments you made on an earlier version has been taken into account and in which not even the typos that you painstakingly listed have been corrected.

- The author chose this particular journal for a second attempt in response to a suggestion made in your first report and you feel a certain responsibility for having encouraged this submission.

- You have a knowledge of the subject few others share, and the associate editor may want to hear your opinion anyway. One could argue, of course, that if so few people are qualified to referee a given work that different journal editors have to use the same referees, it probably isn't a significant contribution to the field. I do not really agree. An editor may feel that there are only a few individuals who can be trusted with writing a good report. That does not mean that, with time, the article might not gain readers and eventually have some impact.[6]

- If you initially recommended rejection of a paper mainly because it was not "to your taste," it may be more natural for you to decline the assignment than if your criticisms had to do with such issues as the correctness of the analysis or the quality of the scholarship. In these latter cases, a quick look at the paper will tell you whether the problems you noted in your first report have been addressed. If they have not, you will save everybody precious time by sending a revised report that takes into account whatever changes have been made in the paper.

If you were in favor of publication but the paper was rejected anyway, you will certainly welcome the opportunity to have your opinion heard again, and few people would object. However, if you do accept a second refereeing job on the same paper, let the associate editor know that it is your second time. In your cover letter, explain your earlier involvement with the work. There are several ways in which editors can use your assessment in this situation. They can put it aside, use it informally as an additional input into their own opinion, or treat it as a regular report. Let the individual editor decide.

- *You are concerned about meeting the deadline suggested by the associate editor.* Being occasionally late by two or three weeks is not a major problem though. In our discipline, the publishing process is rather slow—as you have probably already discovered when submitting your own work. On the other hand, being deliberately slow to avoid receiving additional assignments too soon is not the best use of your

---

6. Hamermesh (1992) disagrees with me on this issue.

knowledge of game theory. Try to do a little better than the average referee; the associate editor and the author will be grateful.[7] But if you have received so many refereeing requests that you risk being swamped—and this may happen sooner after you graduate than you expect—you certainly have the right to say no. In fact, you should. Do not let refereeing work hurt your own research.

On occasion, you may accept an assignment but have to postpone your evaluation of a paper because the author did not include all the proofs, or the article is based on some earlier work that is unpublished or not readily available. Get the material you need from the library, a colleague, or the author's web page. In some (rare) cases, you may have to write to the associate editor and request that the author make certain items available to you.

If you decide to decline an assignment, the sooner the better. So, quickly assess the paper when you receive it. Anywhere from a few minutes to half an hour should suffice to make up your mind. If you let it sit on your desk only to discover several weeks later that you have to turn down the job, you will have caused unnecessary delay. Or, out of guilt for this delay, you may do the work anyway. But if you had good reasons to decline it in the first place, they probably still apply and you will not write a good report. Acting quickly is also important if, as discussed earlier, you need additional material that may take time to obtain. You do not want to discover a whole two months after receiving the assignment that you absolutely have to consult a related discussion paper by the author or a paper published in a journal to which your library does not subscribe.

8   Benefits to You of Your Refereeing Work

Take your refereeing jobs seriously. Refereeing appears to be a very unrewarding activity: essentially only one person, the associate editor, knows who produced this thoughtful report. However, the job is part of your service to the profession. It does have a cost, but your turn will come to be the beneficiary. And even from the selfish viewpoint of your own preferences, your efforts will not be in vain. By repeatedly doing a good job you are helping your reputation; editors talk to each other

---

7. Hamermesh (1994) is a good source of information on what the usual delays are. He also discusses in detail the sociology of refereeing.

and to other members of the profession. The quality of refereeing is often mentioned in recommendation letters written on behalf of young researchers. Your work will eventually earn you a spot on a board of editors, giving you more of a chance to make your opinion count.

Another benefit of refereeing is that it helps you keep up with the literature. Next to presenting a paper in a class, there is nothing like refereeing it to become really familiar with it. This in-depth work will be very useful to your own research.

9 References

Eckel, Catherine. "Writing Reviews for the Economics Program at the National Science Foundation That Will Make Your Program Officer Love You." *Committee on the Status of Women in the Economics Professions Newsletter* (Winter 1999): 11–12.

Hamermesh, Daniel S. "The Young Economist's Guide to Professional Etiquette." *Journal of Economic Perspectives* 6 (1992): 169–79.

———. "Facts and Myths about Refereeing." *Journal of Economic Perspectives* 8 (1994): 153–63.